PAPUA NEW GUINEA

Mama Graun

Reading Texts for Grades 6–8

John Kian

OXFORD

Level 8, 737 Bourke Street, Docklands, Victoria 3008, Australia

Oxford University Press is a department of the University of Oxford. It furthers the University's objective of excellence in research, scholarship, and education by publishing worldwide in

Oxford New York

Auckland Cape Town Dar es Salaam Hong Kong Karachi
Kuala Lumpur Madrid Melbourne Mexico City Nairobi
New Delhi Shanghai Taipei Toronto

With offices in

Argentina Austria Brazil Chile Czech Republic France Greece
Guatemala Hungary Italy Japan Poland Portugal Singapore
South Korea Switzerland Thailand Turkey Ukraine Vietnam

OXFORD is a trademark of Oxford University Press in the UK and in certain other countries

First published 2006
Reprinted 2009, 2010, 2023 (D)

ISBN 978 0 19 555347 5

Typeset by Pier Vido Design
Printed and bound in Australia by Ligare Book Printers Pty Ltd

Acknowledgment
This book was developed with the support of the Australian Government through the Curriculum Reform Implementation Project.

Contents

Introduction

This book supports the Language Outcomes for Grades 6, 7 and 8 by supplying a variety of text types that meet the needs of the Language outcomes for Grades 6–8.

These texts have been organised under the theme of 'Mama Graun' (Mother Earth) and have strong links to the Social Science and Science subjects of the Grades 6, 7 and 8 syllabuses. The Mama Graun theme was chosen because of its central importance to life.

> *Do you realise that Mama Graun takes care of her own? Humans cut the trees down for logging and unnecessarily burn up the grass and savannah grasslands. When mining for natural treasures, we damage the land, sometimes so extensively that animals or plant life can no longer survive on such barren land. This is sad, and it is a fact that if PNG continues to flout our natural resources such as timber, gold, copper, oil, fish and other treasures of this beautiful island country, in the next century we will face a drastic shortage.*

This book contains a range of texts about real and imaginary worlds related to the Mama Graun theme using the following genres:

Narratives—texts that include myths, legends, short fictional stories

Recounts—texts that recall a series of events

Reports—texts that describe a specific object, creature, or natural phenomena

Procedures—texts that explain how to achieve an outcome through a sequence of steps

Explanations—texts that describe in scientific terms how natural and technological phenomena came into being

Expositions—texts that try to convince the reader that what the writer is saying is true

Poetry—texts that help us think about familiar things in different ways. Poetry uses language, rhythm, rhyme and structure to capture the essence of a feeling, thought, object or scene.

At the end of each text there is a 'Things to do after reading' section which consists of activities that allow students to respond to the specific text using the other modes of language, namely: Speaking and Listening and Writing.

John Kian

Narrative

1

The legend of the two sister lakes: Lai and Ambum

Once upon a time in the great forest of Wapimanda, lay two famous lakes side by side. One was called Lai and the other Ambum. They were sister lakes. The two lakes spent their days lazing around the trees and talking to the possums and the other animals.

At night they watched the yellow moon swimming lazily across the sky, and the brilliant stars twinkling in the Milky Way. The two lakes let the animals drink from their bosoms, enjoying the tickling feeling of the creatures' tongues on their nipples.

However, the two lakes had very different temperaments. Lai was a noisy pool. She liked to jump up and splash against the reeds and the banks of the forest whenever a breeze blew. Ambum on the other hand, liked to lie quietly and listen to the birds and animals of the forest singing their beautiful melodies.

One day, as the two sisters were gossiping, Lai suddenly said, 'I think we should go away from this part of the forest. Let's run away very early tomorrow, so that no one will see us go. We can travel all the way down and join up with the river that flows to the sea. Together we can go with him to see the sky meets the earth! What do you think, sis?'

'Uh, but why?' asked Ambum puzzled. 'We are fine here and I like living here!' and she stretched stifling a yawn. 'It's kind of peaceful here and besides, the animals are friendly. Err, why do you want us to move, Lai?'

Lai replied. 'I know it's peaceful and quiet here, but don't you have a sense of adventure? Wouldn't you like to see new places and meet other lakes and rivers? Just think about it, if we don't like the adventure, we can always come back!'

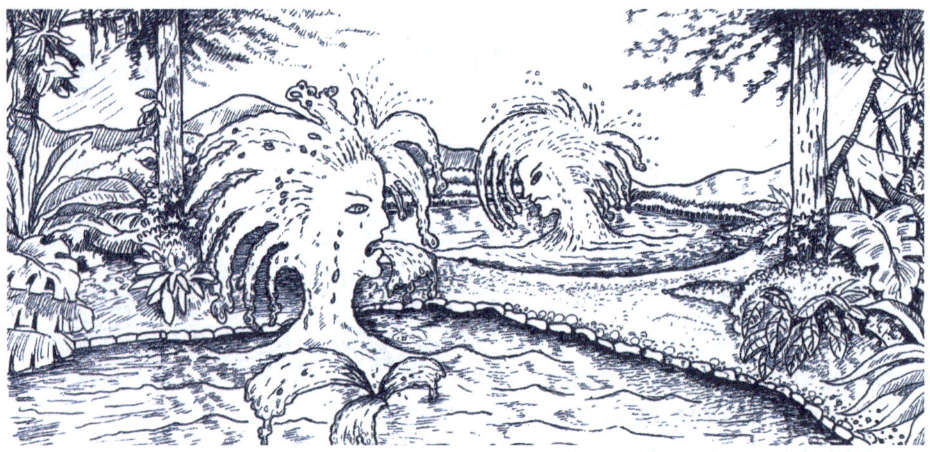

'Well, I don't know about that. Uh—I mean I don't know whether we can come back!' frowned Ambum. 'But I sure like the idea of an adventure.'

'Yeah. Think of the places we will see,' urged Lai, and rolled her belly, causing the fishes to run for shelter. 'You never know. We might find another beautiful place.'

Ambum did not like the idea of leaving, but the thought of an adventure tickled her fancy. 'Yeah, why not? Let us go early tomorrow morning. But, remember Lai, please no tricks! We have to move silently and no touching people's food gardens or houses. Is that understood?'

'No noise! No touching food gardens and people's houses, I promise!' Lai said quickly. Then again shook her belly in mirth, and the waters splashed over the banks, even though there was no breeze. The people in the villages heard the thunder-like noise and were frightened. 'Hey, what's happening up there?' some asked.

'I think Lai is grumbling as always!' said one villager.

'Beware!' warned an old man. 'The time of parting is at hand!' and he walked away before others could ask him any questions. People wondered what was happening up in the mountains, as they went on their way, working and hunting.

Ambum was not happy. 'Shsssh woman! Keep the noise down. We don't want to frighten the people,' she chided, 'and besides you promised! Didn't you, Lai?'

The flora and fauna of the forest heard the two lakes discussing their departure. The birds were sad because their natural swimming and feeding habitat would be there no more. The catfish in the bottom of the lake said to his mate the eel fish, 'Did you hear what the two were discussing? Uh, what's going to happen to us?'

Up above, the eagle heard it too and said to the earth. 'Please, mother of the universe. Can you not stop the two lakes from moving?'

'That's right,' said the furred marsupial. 'Can't you stop them?'

'Why do they want to go?' asked the kingfishers. 'Don't they like it here?'

Mama Graun smiled at the animals and the stunning flora that grew around the lake. Yes, it was true that the animals would miss the waters. But she had no power to stop the lakes from leaving. 'I know what you are all thinking. I'll try to do my best. But I can't stop the waters from moving, friends!'

'Uh, what can we do? If there is no water here, how will the fish in the lake survive?' said the green parrot with the yellow beak.

The eagle said, 'They will probably perish unless a miracle happens!' and shook her noble head sadly.

Mama Graun listened and was frustrated, not knowing what to do. It was really the right of any living things to move and live where they wanted. Even as the mother of the earth, she had no power over the natural world. She was also part of the great circle of life. The animals, the people and the plants all depended on each other for survival.

'Hey, Mama Graun. A penny for your thoughts,' said a deep rumbling voice.

Mama Graun looked up startled and saw Skyman had come down and was watching her with a puzzled expression. 'Uh, is my face that transparent even for you to see from way above?' she asked with a frown.

'Well, you seem worried. Is anything the matter, Mama Graun?'

'Thanks for your concern, Skyman. It's nothing I can't handle,' she said with a sad smile. 'The two lakes, Lai and Ambum, have decided to go on a journey and I don't know what's going to happen to some of the animals that live and feed from them! I am kind of worried, kind sir.'

'Oh, is that so? Well, they have the right to move, I guess. You really can't stop them, can you?'

'No, I don't want to do that, sir!'

'Hey, wait a minute. I have an idea!' smiled Skyman, and instantly the whole universe brightened with a brilliant glow of assorted colours.

'Wow, look at the stars!' said the possum. 'The milky way is lit up like Christmas night!'

'Phew!' sighed the miok. 'Something good must be happening, up there.'

'Oh yes. And what a beauty! I wish it was like this all the time!' said the owl wistfully.

Skyman heard the commentary and switched on the whole heavens. Brilliant stars lit up everywhere, even deep into the galaxies where natural eyes could not observe. It was so gorgeous watching all the wonderful colours of the rainbow being displayed in the Milky Way. Even humans stood and paused to watch the magnificent display of brilliant colours in the universe.

'Haw man. Stop showing off and tell me what you think, kind sir.' asked Earth woman with a sly grin.

'Uh, sorry ma'am. I was just lighting my world—'

'Yeah, well, I like it too! But we are talking about the lives of the fish and water insects, sir. Can you help?'

'That's not a problem, Mama Graun. As soon as they take off, I'll open the skies and fill up the lakes again! How does that sound, eh?'

'That's great, sir. Oh, Skyman, you are really something. 'But please, direct all rain to the Wapai Mountains. I'll then direct all the water into one channel to fill up the lakes,' and she smiled cheerfully. 'Oh man, I feel great. Thanks Skyman. You are always there to help!'

'It's no big deal, ma'am. After all we are part of the great circle of the universe. We all depend on each other. Perhaps, one day I'll call on a favour,' Skyman said as he retreated into the heavens. Mama Graun sat and thought about the lives she and Skyman supported. She felt good that life was preserved on the earth. No loss of life would occur unnecessarily.

Lai and Ambum were too busy discussing their own plans and did not think about the consequences of their actions. For centuries they had been in the mountains supporting and sustaining the lives of the animals, the fishes and the natural environment. They were going to leave all these behind and go away.

'Wow, think of all the new places we will see!' Lai said excitedly. Then she paused in thought. 'Eh-r-r, do you know what's at the end of where the sky meets the land?'

'Gee, come to think of it, I know nothing!' said Ambum. 'Why don't we ask the eagle? He might know.'

Lai moved about trying to locate the eagle. She saw the magnificent bird sitting high up on his favourite treetop. 'Hey Iakepam (eagle)?' yelled Lai rudely. 'Do you know anything about the place where the land meets the sky?'

'Why do you ask?' said the eagle innocently.

'That's none of your business—' glowered Lai.

'Please, Iakepam. We are thinking of going on an adventure to see the place where the sky meets the land for ourselves. Can you help us?' Ambum asked politely.

'Going for a trip, are you?' asked the cassowary, walking up to Lai's sides. 'If you go, you can't come back! You know that, don't you?'

'Don't we know that moron!' said Lai rudely. 'Get off from my side, you two-legged fruit sucking, long necked—' but was stopped in mid-sentence abruptly.

The cassowary stretched its long legs and jabbed Lai's side with a lightning kick.

'Hey, that hurts!' and Lai tried to grab the cassowary but it stepped onto higher ground with ease. Lai roared with fury. 'I'll get you next time—' she cried in fury.

'Ohoo, do shut up, flat belly,' said the eagle. 'At least we'll be glad you will not come back,' he muttered under his breath.

'Did you say something, foul-smelling dung eater!' fumed Lai again.

'Shut up!' roared Ambum. 'One man's food is another man's poison! No need to get rude, Lai!'

But Lai fumed and rolled all over the enbankment, shaking its mighty belly, rolling water to heights it never went. The grass and trees and animals held their breath. They did not want to anger the foul-mouthed lake.

'Thanks Ambum!' said the eagle. 'I hear the journey is long and dangerous. But you know that if you leave here, there is no way of coming back, uh?'

'We know that and thank you for your warning! When I go, I'll leave a bit of me here so that it will remind you of me.' Ambum said sadly. 'But Lai, your promise. Will you keep it? If you can't, I won't—'

'Ahiee, I'm sorry sister.' Lai apologised. 'Yep, I'll keep the promise. Don't you worry, girl!' she said innocently.

'Thanks sister. Tomorrow you travel east and I'll travel west. We'll meet at Lege, okay?' said Ambum as she moved off to share the news with her friends.

'That's fine with me. We'll meet at Lege and travel down together!'

'Wow, isn't it great! We are finally going to move!' laughed the tadpole jumping up and down happily. 'I can't wait to see great new places!'

'Don't be too sure about that friend,' warned the eel. 'Lai can be cruel. She will more likely take a short cut!'

'A short cut? But, why? It's not a race!' said the green frog, sitting on a stunning water lily with breathtaking pink colours.

'Well, you know her. She doesn't need a reason' said the catfish.

A brown frog wallowing under a crack in the rock jumped into the water. 'I just overheard the two quarrelling on this issue. Those of you that want to go with them, be very careful. You could get hurt!'

'Thanks for the information,' said the eel.

Mama Graun rumbled and all the living things paused to listen. 'Yes, the two sisters will travel with the first light tomorrow. But don't worry. Ambum has promised to leave some water. And help is coming from above. Make sure all the animals find a good shelter for at least a day or two. Rain—and I mean heavy rain—will pour down here!'

'Is Skyman going to help?' asked the eagle.

'Yes, and we are thankful to him. Just stay out of sight. You will have new lakes in no time!'

'Thanks for your help, Mama Graun. We owe you one!' said the eagle. 'And thanks to the Skyman too!'

The two lakes did not pay much attention to the conversation that was going around them. They were busy. Ambum spent the evening farewelling all her friends. She promised that she would leave a small part of her water for the animals and the forest to drink from. No one said anything because they all felt sad. Lai on the other hand, secretly made plans to take the fastest

route and shortest way to her destination. She was not going to keep her promise about going carefully.

Thus early the next morning, before the crack of dawn the two lakes set out on their adventure. Lai set off first. She gave very little thought to the agreement they had reached. Being considerate to people and the environment was not in her vocabulary. Instead, she swept down as fast as she could, destroying food gardens, houses and even murdering people. She pushed down trees and just about anything that stood in her path. Lai was very destructive.

People cried in grief and anger. 'Why is Lai always hurting us?'

'She is self-centred and selfish!'

'She washed down my house! I have no home to live in!' wailed a mother.

Lai only laughed at their misery and continued her destructive journey.

'Where is my dad? Please, find my dad!' cried one small boy.

The people grew very angry with Lai. 'Make her dirty all the time, people. Drop your waste in the water. Make her look ugly!' they chanted.

'No! No, I can't see—' cried Lai. But no one showed any mercy. As she passed, people threw rubbish and made Lai as dirty and filthy as was possible. Lai was mad but the people wised up and moved to higher ground.

Meanwhile, Ambum chose her way carefully. When travelling down the mountain and valleys she was always careful not to touch people's houses and food gardens nor to damage the rain-forest. She made sure that she only passed through areas where very little damage, if any, was done on land inhabited by people and animals. Every time she came upon a village or a food garden, she moved around them. Thus, it took her longer to reach the river where she was to join together with Lai to reach their destination. Finally, it was nightfall when Ambum arrived at the end of the journey and to her surprise, saw Lai already at Lege.

As Ambum came up, Lai called out, 'Hey, there. How come it took you so long? It's only a short distance!' and she laughed with mirth. 'I have been waiting for hours. I thought you got lost and went in the opposite direction!' she chuckled again.

Ambum cleared her throat, dreading what she knew must have happened. But she was also puzzled. 'How did you get here so fast, my sister?' she managed to ask. 'And uh—what happened to you? You look filthy!'

'What? What filth, eh?' asked Lai examining herself. 'Oh, noo-oo,' she cried.

'Haw, shut up! How long have you waited, sister?'

'Well, now. Let's see!' she calmed down quickly. 'I'd say for about six hours. Oh Ambum! I coursed as fast as I could and straight wherever I could!' and grinned evilly. 'That's how I got here fast!'

'But—But, what about the people? The food gardens, animals and—!' Ambum cried in disbelief. 'The promise—you, uh, promised!' Suddenly she understood. The people had got their revenge and made Lai filthy and ugly looking.

'Oh them?' asked Lai mockingly. 'Well, I heard a few people shouting and some even tried to stop me, but I went right through them! All I did was push a few trees, houses or gardens out of my way!' she said with a mocking laugh.

Ambum was very angry when she heard Lai had destroyed the people's food gardens and homes. She shouted, 'You dirty, filthy, foul-mouthed water! You had no right to destroy innocent lives and homes!' and she charged her sister. The two lakes met head on and the people heard their clash miles around. They knew that Ambum was fighting her sister Lai because she had been cruel. The two sisters began pushing each other and to this day, you can hear the thundering waves at the tributary where the two rivers meet, and journey down to the Sepik River. They have never stopped fighting.

Higher up in the mountains forest, Skyman opened his doors and rain fell in heavy torrents. It rained and rained for three whole days. Mama Graun directed all the water in a single burrow to the near empty lakes and filled

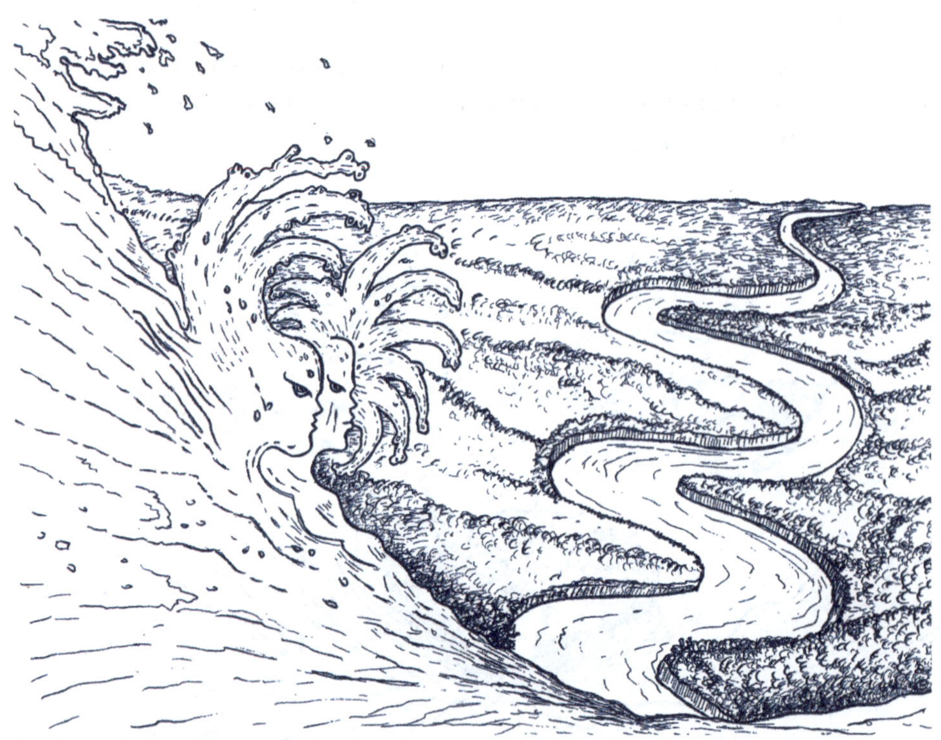

them up for the animals to survive. Together the two great bodies of the universe cooperated to save some of the lives of the animals on Earth. The people living in the area also heard the rain but strangely enough, they saw no floods or streams carrying flooded water down the valley. It seemed like the water had just dried up in the mountains.

Today, whenever Lai floods, it always destroys food gardens and kills people and animals. Ambum seldom floods and when it does, it is always careful not to destroy food gardens or hurt people.

Things to do after reading

Activity 1

Answer the following questions in full sentences.

- Are Lai and Ambum human beings?
- Why did the two sisters decide to move?
- Which river was the gentle one?
- What does having different temperaments mean?
- Where are these two rivers found?

Activity 2

Fill in the missing blanks with the appropriate word from your vocabulary list.

Ambum was ________________ as to how quickly Lai had travelled. (tickled, puzzled or speechless)

Ambum ______________________ that Lai would be respectful of the food gardens, homes, people and animals when they left their location. (understood, thought or agreed)

Lai _____________________ so fast that she ___________________ everything that got in its way. (swam, travelled, ran) (destroyed, moved, swept away)

_________________ was angry because _____________ had not kept her side of the agreement. (Lai, Ambum, the people)

Where two rivers come and meet is called a _________________. (tributary, junction or estuary)

Activity 3

Develop your critical thinking

Animals seem to be far more clever than humans. They know when to protect their own species. What is the lesson behind this story? Why are stories told using non-human characters? For example, take the story of the lakes. Could they have really talked? Why or why not? Write your explanations in a paragraph form. Think of your own fantasy stories and write about them.

Recount

The great spear gun

I remember this like it was yesterday. I ran lightly down the side of Senake Street, past the Smugglers Inn and entered the road leading to the famous Lighthouse of beautiful Madang. It was a lovely day, with a cool southerly breeze blowing against me, coming in from the Bismarck Sea. 'Only a kilometre to go,' I thought as I jogged towards my destination. I lengthened my stride knowing the end was near. I was physically fit, even for a twenty-year-old lad. As I increased my speed, I instantly felt the tightening of my muscles and upsurge in my heart rate. I felt good. If I wanted to, I could sprint down to the lighthouse and experience no fatigue. This was my usual run that took me around the tip of Astrolabe Bay, and back to the college, where I was a student in scientist.

Usually, I did a non-stop ten kilometre run around the Astrolabe Bay, the Kalibobo Lighthouse, along the beach and back to the college. But today was different. The whole family, my father and my twin sisters and even my mother, were down at Machine Gun Beach to visit. My mother is studying at the local university, and had come for her study break. Machine Gun Beach is situated just below the lighthouse, near 'sip pia'—a name given to the old burnt out Japanese warship—which was destroyed during World War II. Last night, the

family had decided that we would have our picnic at the beach, a favourite swimming spot for the girls. I told them I would join them after lunch because I had a class to attend.

Now I was on my way. I increased my tempo, as I got closer. Sweat poured down all over me like sweet rain but I did not mind. I liked the sweat and the physical endurance of exercise. With a lifetime of running marathons, I was sound mentally and physically. For some unknown reason, or as I guessed a biological mishap, I possessed great strength. I could effortlessly pick up two 50 kilogram coffee bags, 50 kilogram in one hand and 50 kilogram in my other hand, and with a quick jerk, put them in an open back truck with ease.

One time, when I was 15, we had no jack for a flat tyre.

'Jake, can you lift the truck so that I can put this tyre back?' my father had asked gently.

'But—but Dad?' I had replied puzzled, looking at him with a frown.

'Son, I know you can to do it!' he had said staring me in the eye.

I had hesitated not knowing what to do. I had been scared and confused.

'Please Jake. You can do it! Here, lift from this end, here— ' and showed me where and how to lift the three ton truck. Gosh, to my surprise I did lift the tail end of the truck, with some exertion but it was manageable, and my father put the tyres back. After that experience, I was embarrassed with my strength and kept it a secret. Only a few friends knew of my extraordinary strength and they were sworn not to reveal the secret to anyone.

I turned right on Able Street and 20 metres down I saw where my dad had parked the truck. I increased speed, my legs pumping, feeling no fatigue. I reached the picnic area and as I turned the corner, I heard the twins yelling excitedly. They had seen me. 'Jake, Ja-ke-ee' they called, making enough noise for all the beach goers to notice. 'Come on, you big-for-nothing' yelled Shannan.

'Over here,' I could hear Emerald calling. She was swimming with some of her girlfriends. I guess she just wanted to show me off to her friends. I grinned as I thought about it. Some of the girls were very beautiful.

The twins were 15 or nearly 16. By November they would be 16 years old. Emerald was the gentle one. Shannan was quite opposite. I always thought that Shannan should have been a male. She was always getting into trouble in school for beating up boys who were much older than her. She even played rugby tackle with the village boys, and the lads called her 'man body', meaning she had a male body, which was understandable. Even at 15 she was tall and muscular. There was no sign of any female development yet, which our grandmother said was not unusual. Her mother had had a similar build. Grandma said she vividly recalled that her mum was a giant of a woman. She often told us fascinating stories about her mother leading men into battles and even claiming a few scalps, before being forced into an arranged marriage. She said Shannan had the same trait and she was not surprised she had a man's physique!

Shannan was the rebel in the family. She challenged me all the time and sometimes we traded blows. I was gentle with her, but oh boy, she would try to beat the hell out of me. Only my great strength and speed prevented me from ending up with broken teeth or black eyes. In the village and also at school, she was respected and no one made fun of her. But they were both my baby sisters and I loved them dearly. I grinned as I heard the girls yelling happily.

I reached the truck and looked inside to locate where Dad had put my spear gun.

'It's under the left side seat in the back,' called out my father. He knew what I was looking for. I opened the back doors of the Toyota 10-seater and carefully took out my invention.

It was a spear gun and quite unique. I sensed it held magical powers within. At least I thought so, smiling to myself. I had designed and crafted it, spending countless hours, making it perfect. The steel end was made of reinforced steel and it was longer than my arms. For the front end, I had specially designed four spiked sharp steel rods, each protruding symmetrically in four directions. On each of these rods, I had designed special spikes, so that if they entered a large fish, it had no way of shaking itself free.

And to free the spikes I had designed a lever. When you pressed hard on this lever, the spikes withdrew, allowing you to pull the spear free without damaging the fish. It was of superior craftsmanship and I had hardly used it before, except for a number of trials on banana trunks. Today, of all days, I had asked Dad to bring the spear gun along.

I extracted the fishing weapon and tested the rubber for tension and damages. There was none. The polished *kwila* handle of teak shined. Next I checked the release switch. It worked perfectly. Satisfied, I turned to the beach. Shannan saw me coming and yelled, 'I'll race you to the wreck, big-for-nothing,' and laughing, began swimming towards the shipwreck. She knew I would be angry when she teased me like that.

'Shannan, please wait for your brother.' yelled mum. But she was already out of earshot.

Dad also tried. 'Hey, wait for your brother? It could be dangerous!'

'Hey, harim tok, man body,' one of her girlfriend's teased.

Getting no response, Emerald volunteered. 'Hey, wait up, sis? We'll race together,' and her girlfriends swam after Shannan.

As I walked towards the beach I noticed quite a large number of beach goers. Many of the people I knew. But there were also strangers on the beach, enjoying themselves just like my family.

Tony, a schoolmate of Shannan's, asked, 'You're not going to take up that silly challenge, are you?'

'Well, I don't know, Tony. It's not important, is it?'

'Well, not to you bro, but I know your sister,' he said grinning.

I laughed knowing Tony had a crush for Shannan,

'Do you think she heard the calls for her to stop?' he asked with a frown.

'And do you think she would have stopped?' I asked raising my eyebrows.

'Silly girl!' he said fondly.

I shook my heard grinning. I knew my kid sister well. Even if she had heard she would not have listened. I quickened my stride down to the beach intending to ignore her challenge. But a victory for her was my misery. I looked out to sea and saw that she was too far ahead, even for me to catch up and I was the best. But a lot of people were also chasing her. 'That's good. It will keep her busy!'

'She's too far Jake!' said Dad coming up. 'I don't think you can catch her.'

Suddenly, I knew what to do. I bolted.

Instead of entering the water, I ran along the beach and reached a small bush track. Without breaking my stride, I sped up the small incline and entered the thin foliage. Normally I would fear the snakes, lizards, frogs and millipedes that crawled around this area, but today I was in a hurry. My feet crushed any living things that I came across in my haste to take the short cut that I knew would take me directly to the wreck.

'I can still beat my sister,' I deliberated as I ran.

'Ouch, he's stepped on my legs,' wailed a tiny voice.

'Hey, watch where you are going!' yelled another voice angrily. It was a snail.

'Run! Run and hide under the log—Oops, just in time!' said the lizard as it crawled under a rotten oak tree trunk.

'What's got into him?' retorted the hornbill perched on a coconut tree.

'He's running a race,' said the seagulls, gliding past me with ease.

'Hey, did I hear voices?' I asked myself as I plunged through the undergrowth effortlessly, leaping over fallen logs and mud puddles. The spear gun was still in my hands.

'Hey, magic *supia*, why don't you do something? Send him a signal or something,' suggested the casuarina tree.

'It's not time yet!' echoed a magical figure as it materialised out of the spear gun. I was unaware of the change. The figure, a pot-bellied, chubby old man, majestically appeared. His appearance was like Buddha but instead of a shaped head, this magical image's hair was held in place by a Highlander's wig.

'The man can't hear us now, b-u-ut h-e will so-on! He cert-ainly w-ill so-oo-on!' slurred the wise owl with sleepy eyes.

A few of the forest animals tried to see what was happening out in the ocean.

'Come on. Let's go to the beach. I want to see the great battle,' said the tortoise.

I sensed something was happening to me but I still couldn't figure it out. I tipped a rise, overlooking the inlet to the bay, and saw a number of water splashes scattered along the bay. 'Good. Other swimmers had taken the challenge.' I grinned, happy that she was not alone. But I did notice that one

lone figure was drawing closer to the wreck. 'Oh man,' I uttered in dismay. With a curse I took off once more. From the next rise, I knew I would actually get a better view and assess my chances.

'If he doesn't hurry, he won't save his sister,' said the white and brown coloured possum from the treetop. 'I can see the danger!'

'That's what we are trying to tell him but he won't listen,' said a seagull flying low near my face. The gull flapped its wings and screeched but I paid no attention.

'Fly closer to his face, sir,' said the lizard.

'No, leave him be!' roared Mama Graun. 'From here on, I will handle him!'

'That's fair enough,' said the mango tree. 'I can't move. But I sure as hell can stretch myself,' and the mango tree began to reach for the sky, until it could almost touch the heavens. 'Now, I can see the ocean!' and birds flew to perch on its branches to witness the skirmish.

I still did not know what was happening around me. Above me, I saw hundreds of seagulls who had launched themselves from the treetops, boulders and the cliff edges, swaying idly, legs trussed back and wings motionless, cupping the air. Those closer to the cliff tops screeched noisily, some flying low down touching the rapidly moving black fin, trying to redirect its course. Others sensed the danger and wings flapped about screaming to be heard. The foaming waters crashed against the sheer cliffs, seething foam and hissing to shake off the fear of the unknown threat that the ocean felt it was responsible for bringing.

I could hear the voices of the other swimmers calling to their friends. 'She is going to win!'

'No, he's going to win!' cried a female voice.

'Yes, her brother took a short cut. He's going to come first!' yelled another female voice.

There was laughter and cheering all along the beach. The crowd were enjoying themselves. They all liked watching a challenge, particularly where females were involved.

I reached the crest and searched quickly for my sister. From here it was just a step away. I would reach the wreck first if she had not done so by now. I saw her about 20 metres from the wreck. She had taken the deep-end of the inlet, trying to get to the platform, cutting off my entry. But I calculated that I still had a chance. I grinned and my eyes followed the inlet out to the open ocean and my heart stopped beating.

I blinked once, not believing my eyes. 'Are my eyes seeing things?' I asked myself. I blinked again and quickly rubbed both eyes to see clearly. 'Oh no ' I whispered and drew in my breath. A dark lengthy shape with a protruding black fin was swimming near the wreck. I could tell immediately that it was a shark circling around waiting for an easy prey. There was no doubt in my mind that the shark would attack Shannan. I didn't wait.

'Shark! Shark, Shannan!' I yelled, jumping up and down. No one heard me. 'I'm too far away,' As I ran, I yelled, 'Shark, Shark in th-ee, wa-at-ter,' but no sound came from my lips. I waved and pointed frantically but no one saw me. I sprinted. I sprinted like I had never run before in my whole life. My body responded to years of training and I ran with blinding speed. I knew deep down that the shark would attack my sister as she tried to reach the platform. 'A shark! But— how? How had it come close to the shores' These questions flipped over and over in my mind as I raced down.

Under the sea, all the sea creatures saw the monster's purpose but they were powerless to do anything. The shark was the king of the deep and no one dared challenge him. They stood in stony silence as the drama unfolded.

'Can't we—?' a young dolphin asked eagerly.

'Shsssh! Keep your month shut, son,' uttered mother dolphin through her teeth.

'Did I hear something?' roared the great white shark.

'Nay! Oh—oh, great king of the deep!' said the octopus.

'Good,' warned the shark as it swam around. 'My dinner is coming!'

I knew that there was an overhang over the water where children often jumped off into the bay. I aimed for that very spot. In my mind I could clearly visualise what I was going to do. 'If only I can get between my sister and the shark in time, I could distract it long enough for me to prepare my spear gun.'

I was about five metres away from the overhang, when I saw the shark make its first attack. Like a slow motion picture, I saw the shark dive and with a flip of its mighty tail, it aimed straight for Shannan. 'Shannan! Shannan a shark!' I yelled but again no sound came forth. Suddenly a strange phenomenon took over me. I felt my body moving into another shape. I sensed my body change and become another second being, with greater strength and senses, someone like Superman or Flash Gordon. I could see and hear things I ordinarily would not have. I was able to feel the waves rushing against the shores. I heard the mighty ocean cry in agony as it brought its message of death.

'Dive! Dive sis! Shannan dive, for God's sake, dive!' I yelled frantically, still running. In that same instance, Shannan saw the shark's fin as it swam directly for her. She looked up straight into my eyes and even from this great distance I could tell that there was no panic, no fear, just an icy calmness in her. I was proud of her. She dived.

'The girl's diving! We'll try to distract the shark from above,' and a bunch of seagulls went towards the moving shark. The seagulls swooped down, their sharp beaks causing havoc on the shark's fin but the huge beast did not alter its course of destruction.

I heard the birds talk. But I did not stop my momentum. I ran at that same blinding speed and leaped into the sea, like an Olympic long jumper. 'Here, let me give you a push,' and I found Mama Graun, lifting me up and hurling me far out into the bay. Like an eagle in the sky, I glided over the cliff.

A shark's attack is very swift and brutal. Very few humans live to tell the tale. Just a flick of its powerful tail and it will be upon you before you can blink an eye. Sharks have highly sensitive senses, but normal eyes like you and me. Luckily for Shannan, her swimming costume was a fatigue suit: specially designed swimwear that can camouflage a swimmer in the ocean.

'Shannan, don't move! Just let your legs keep you swimming,' I whispered. She stared in my direction sensing my presence. I was sending messages of warning from way above and it was only for a second but time seemed to stand still for us.

She responded, 'Jake? I'm sorry, uh,' and tried to apologise.

'Hey kid, don't apologise. The shark is turning and it's hungry, sister. I can sense the beast's stomach churning.'

'Is it, brother? I'll try to hold it off as long as I can. But, if I can't, well—' and left the sentence unfinished.

'Shsssh! Think positive sister. I know you can do it. — Oh yes, I know!' We were conversing telepathically, a form of sending messages through the mind. 'Hey, that was great.' I grinned as I sensed my power to do these extraordinary feats. I found I could talk to the animals of the sea in their own language. It was pure magic but I was not alone. There was another.

Strangely, the face of an old man, wise in his years appeared in front of me and directed all the movements my body performed. It was like the Ali Baba and magic lamp story, in which the Giant Genie comes out to help Ali Baba when he rubs the magic lamp. In my case, the strange old ghoul seemed to be living in my spear gun.

A seagull swooped down and danced in my face, its wings swinging systematically. 'The creature is a bad one. It has claimed a lot of lives, friend. Beware, for it knows a lot of tricks.'

The mysterious ancient face added, 'It is told that a day will come when the sea and the land will meet. Perhaps today is that day.'

I didn't understand what this was all about. I was too confused. But I guessed, it wasn't really me out there. Yet, my body was performing wonders only seen in movies of those super heroes.

Another seagull flew close. 'Hey, the man is descending too fast. He won't have enough time to meet the creature and stop it!'

The lead seagull realised that the other bird was telling the truth. 'You're right Koni dove. Call the others to come. We have to help him.'

'Hey guys, I'm grateful for your suggestions but how can you slow my descent?' I asked, puzzled. For an answer, hundreds of gulls flew towards my body and positioned themselves, under my arms, my legs, and any place they could find a foot or beak hold. Some birds even grabbed my hair. As soon as they got a grip, the birds started to flap their wings, creating a wind force, which instinctively slowed down my plunge into the ocean. The wonderful birds held me up.

It was a fascinating display of bird power. 'Uh-uuu, look at that!' shouted one man pointing his finger at the unbelievable sight.

'Where? I can't see it!' a man asked, searching for the scene.

'A lot of seagulls seem to be flying in one spot over the bay. Maybe they have spotted a school of fish, uh?' said a young *kange*.

'Yeah? But, where? I can't see, sir,' spoke a beautiful lass. 'I can hear the cry of the seagulls but what are they doing?'

'I don't know, ma'am. The sun's rays are shielding the action, man,' said a young man.

'It's magic, sir. I believe what we are seeing is really magic,' said an old man.

'Yes, it is!' and people held their breaths. A hush went up in the crowd. For some strange reason, only a handful of people saw the magical scene. I heard all the questions and conversations as clearly as if I was standing beside the people. I smelled the people's fear and terror. But, I was here on a mission.

'Hey, you lumberjack. You foul-mouthed, sabre-tooth slimy fish!' I said and the huge monster halted in her path, but only for a split second.

'I'm not a lumberjack, you two-legged moron,' said the fish and kept moving.

I laughed with glee. 'The damn shark can also talk. Gosh man, we're both talking the same lingo!' I thought excitedly. But I was in no position to have fun. I was concerned for my sister. I could picture accurately what was going to happen.

I taunted again. 'Yes, you are! You slow footed, lumbering mammoth, with broken teeth and ugly lips. You are a coward. Try one of your own for size!' But the shark paid no attention to my jibes.

'Wait, you sneaky, lying, two-faced human. Let me feed on this gorgeous juicy meat. Then I'll attend to you, scum!' said the shark and went ahead to attack my sister. I tried all the ugly words I knew to distract the predator of the deep but I couldn't. I sensed the birds weakening. I was too heavy for them.

Suddenly, the mother of all waters rose up from its depth. 'Can I help?' it hissed, swirling waves, and dancing all around me. But none of its waves, or sprays touched the birds. 'Gosh, the ocean is talking to me too!' I felt all powerful and new strength flowed through me.

The people on the beach saw the rising of the waves and cried out in amazement. 'Look! Look at the waves. They have risen to meet the birds! Uh, what's happening out there?' asked a frightened man.

People pushed each other to take a glimpse of the strange phenomena. For some strange reason, the people had not seen me being lifted and held aloft over the waters, by hundreds of seagulls.

'Please, oh great mother of the sea. I need your help now! Can you just conceal my sister from that foul smelling eater of dead muck?' I asked gently.

'You know, she is wearing that swimsuit. It should help her. The creature has bad eyes, so don't worry!'

'But—but that may be not enough,' I frowned worriedly.

'Believe me it will. There's not much I can do now for her. But for you, yes!'

I watched in fascination, the first attack by the shark. It missed. The deadly creature could not see Shannan clearly. She managed to avoid the first mighty thrust.

I laughed with glee. 'Told you, you would miss her, blind bat!' I taunted.

'Errrr-rrrr-rr,' roared the shark. The powerful teeth crunching, drawing blood forth from its gums. 'Nobody, and I mean nobody, escapes me—' cried the furious monster. The sea swirled and foamed as the great beast made a u-turn. The shark did not know that it had knocked Shannan out with the back swing of its mighty huge tail. Furious at missing its prey, the deadly creature turned for its second assault. Shannan later told us that she was able to avoid the jaws of the first attack, but the back swing of the powerful beast's tail fins knocked her out.

I felt I was the hero, but I was also the bystander, looking at all my actions from above. Without the seagulls' help, the force of the earth's gravity would have pulled me into the ocean. But as it was, I was still suspended above the ocean. I looked down and saw beneath me the shape of the beast and my breath caught in my throat. It was enormous and very, very long too! I calculated it to be about 20 metres or so in length. The monster swiftly turned for its second attempt.

'Ha, ha, you only knocked my sister out, predator,' I taunted. 'Coward! Cheat!'

'Oh, did I really?' grinned the powerful beast as it turned, showing off its jagged teeth. 'I won't miss her a second time—'

'There won't be a second ti-aa-mm-ee!' I roared with fury.

Suddenly, from the depths of the earth, the great Pacific Ocean once more came to my aid. 'Me too, my friend! Me too, if I can help it,' and the ocean swelled. I watched fascinated as it drew in a huge breath, like a diver taking in lungs full of air, ready to dive. The ocean expanded in its size, rattling the fishes and creatures in its depth, causing some to dive for cover.

'Great Ocean, thanks for your help,' I whispered. I got ready for battle. For this was a battle to the death, I knew. Only one of us was going to survive.

The crowd neither saw nor heard any of these conversations. If they had, would they believe it? I doubt it. The crowd's attention was focused on the girl and the mighty shark. I was happy because who in his sane mind, would believe that the Ocean and the animals of the land and sea were talking like human beings?

'Shark attack! A girl is being attacked by a huge shark!' the people screamed.

'Hey, there's a shark in the water!' and people ran everywhere, bumping into each other in panic.

'It's a huge shark,' someone yelled, 'and I think it has missed the girl.'

'It will attack the girl,' and one girl bust into tears. 'She's going to die!'

'Someone, help! Please help?' cried one of Shannan's girlfriends.

Amid the cry for help and rushing about someone had seen us. 'What is that thing up there?' an old man asked pointing in my direction.

'I can't see, with the crazy sun behind, sir,' yelled a bystander. For some strange reason, it seemed the sun played its part and hid the spectacle from the people.

Suddenly, as I hung in the air I saw the dark and sinister shape, swimming directly towards me, at tremendous speed, cutting through the ocean with an effortless grace. Even from up above, I was awed by the display of gigantic power, as it surged towards me at amazing speed, covering the distance in milliseconds. I realised instinctively that we were on a collision course. The birds also realised this. They instinctively switched my position.

The magic spear gun took control or I should say, the pot-bellied, chubby faced Buddha immediately took control. The spear gun now became a live weapon. My arms and the spear gun moved as one. Turning the weapon, I aimed the sharp deadly edge downwards. Then I saw myself raising the weapon high above my head. My muscles tightened and they stood out bulging. There was no panic in my movements.

'He's all yours, sir. Good luck!' and the army of seagulls dropped me like a stone. As I dropped into the ocean, I knew instinctively what to do. I was ready as I entered the deep right above the unsuspecting great beast of the Pacific.

'You should have gone away when I warned you,' I roared.

At the same time, the ocean rose up with an enormous roar. 'Did I not tell you how I was going to help, uh?'

The people heard the rumbling of the great ocean and they retreated in fear. Others stood their ground but felt the churn and thud of the ocean's turmoil, the shock and fear it brought, surging over the reefs, shores and the cliff sides. At the same time, the sea delivered the shark towards the surface, providing it as an offer of sacrifice.

In slow motion, I glimpsed how the creature and my body would come together. My feet were locked firmly together as I entered the water. I made no splash. Instantly, as my warm feet touched the back of the great shark, between its mighty head and first dorsal fin, it reacted. The sudden unexpected contact took the giant creature by surprise. It reared up, turning its great head, the dinner-plate sized eyes rolling madly in their sockets. I felt no fear—just the opposite. My blood soared to greater heights. Instinctively, I saw myself timing the animal's every move in cold precise calculation. As the head reared up, my hands plunged the great spear down into the beast aiming for his heart, with all the strength in my body. The force of the blow was so powerful that the huge creature reared up and stood on its tail in total shock.

The crowd roared in unison as they witnessed the rising of the great creature they now saw and probably would never see again in this lifetime.

Everything seemed to stand still. I saw the fishes in the ocean stay motionless and watch the battle with fascination. They offered no help and I asked for none. The sea having delivered its sacrifice now receded towards Coastwatchers Bay. The seething foam that had hissed and raged against the shores, subsided with the speed of a rushing cyclone, and with a deep sigh, the sea settled back in its habitat.

'Ahiee,' shouted the crowd. 'What is that—huge thing?'

'It's a shark. Look at its size. *Plis, em bikpela tumas, ya?*' cried some. 'Oh, my goodness!'

'Oh, look at that creature. It's a great white shark!' and a shocked stillness went up on the beach.

A great white shark *(Carcharodon carcharias)* was the most feared shark in the Pacific Ocean. There were many tales told of these creatures sinking canoe loads of people and devouring them. And here was a live one rearing up on its mighty tail. On the back and riding on this awesome animal, sat a tiny human form, hanging on to the creature's back for dear life.

'Ahiee, look at that fish hang—' but the man did not finish the sentence.

Again a hush went up in the crowd. 'Magic! It is truly magic!' It was whispered in awe. Others were too shocked to say anything. They stared in awe at the panorama unfolding. The creature was the largest great white shark the people had even seen.

'This is the great battle,' whispered a villager in wonder.

'How in the name of heaven did it get here?' asked one puzzled man.

'It's the fish waste,' said one man immediately.

'What fish waste?' asked another.

'The fish waste from the KM Tuna Cannery!' said the same man. 'The fish cannery has been dumping fish waste into the sea and the smell of blood is bringing sharks here! Just the other day, a crocodile almost ate one boy near the place where the company is dumping the fish waste!'

'Yeah, I heard about that. That's dangerous, isn't it?'

'You don't have to know it's dangerous, man. Just look at that huge great white,' and turned to see what was happening.

'That's right, friends! We never had sharks before in this bay!' shrugged one bystander.

'Yeah. And go over to the waste dump: there are a lot of sharks in those waters, man! Go and see for yourself.' The man moved off to watch the battle between the man and the sea creature.

'Hey, where's the girl?' asked one villager. 'Did the shark eat her?'

Someone replied. 'She's fine. We pulled her out of the water safe but unconscious.'

'Oh no! The shark didn't eat her, sir!' I heard Emerald say. 'My brother saved her! I know he did!' Emerald saw her brother hanging on the back of the great white. 'Oh Mama,' she cried running to her mother.

'Shsssh, my love! Come, let us go check out your sister.' The mother gently but firmly pulled Emerald towards the shore. She knew Shannan would be fine, just like she knew her son was not going to die. Was it a mother's intuition or was it something else? Only she knew the answer.

There was a huge splash again and the crowd geed.

'Kill! Kill, brother! Kill that huge beast. Kilim em. Kill it!' geed the crowd as they watched in awe.

The man and the *Carcharodon carcharias* battled on. It was strange because I could hear every conversation in the crowd. I had an extraordinary power of hearing. The next minute, I felt myself being pulled in a mighty grip down to the ocean bed. For a second I thought I was caught up in the shark's mighty jaws but I felt no pain. Suddenly I realised what was happening. My hands were gripping the spear gun, which was lodged in the head of the awesome creature. I was sitting astride a bucking white, with my feet spread wide and hands holding tightly on to the spear gun.

'Hey lukim,' and the crowd cheered and stared in awe, as many times the huge beast and I surfaced and dived, the beast trying to shake me off.

'Manei, bai dai nao, yea!' said one lady weeping in shock.

'No, em i no nap long dai. Em bai kilim dispela sak, ya, lukim istap,' another flared.

'My son won't die!' said the old man confidently. People standing around him only nodded their heads, not really believing him. They feared the worst.

The great white shark rolled many times trying to shake off the strange two-legged being on its back. When that didn't work, the creature then changed tactics and it shot up into the sky, like a dolphin landing on its back, trying to crush the thing. But it hung on. It death-rolled, it somersaulted in the water, it dived and tried every trick it had accumulated in its lifetime, but to no avail. The people watched in awe. It was just like watching a bucking cowboy on a wild horse, as seen in the movies. I would have loved the thrill of the show, if it was for fun, but I was fighting for my life. Strangely enough, my feet were lodged in the gills of the shark, my toes digging in, securing a firm hold and preventing the shark from breathing properly. This infuriated the monster more and it tossed its mighty head, trying to dislodge the intrusion. But it could not, and the battle raged on. Only one could survive.

The fishes and other creatures in the deep stood still and watched in horror.

The great white shark took its final dive though not as aggressively as before. It was weakening but still ferocious. I hung on. I was being dragged deep into the ocean by a great white shark. I had learned in my science class in grade 6, that the *Carcharodon carcharias* was not a deep-sea shark. It liked living in shallow waters. So immediately, I realised it would not last long under the deep ocean. Even the depth the huge beast was dragging me down to was not beyond a normal human's capability, but I figured it was still dangerous for me. I didn't want to bet my life on the strange events that were taking shape.

Blood was floating everywhere. I knew that the smell of blood would bring other predators. But I held on. Each time the shark moved, my arms propelled the spear deeper and deeper. At the same time, I could feel my lungs almost bursting and the downward pressure of the ocean was getting dangerous. Any minute now, my eardrums would pop.

'Go! Go human to fight another day. For you have now depleted one of my species!' roared the mighty sea, but in a gentle manner.

'I am sorry, mother of the deep. I didn't ask for this—'

'Quiet human. I know your destiny, but hear this. We will meet again and you will know my anger, should you not follow your providence—'

'What destiny, uh?' I tried to ask but no sound came from my lips. Instead I whispered a 'thank you' and using all my strength, I plunged the spear deep into the animal's heart, knowing instinctively that it was the lethal blow. I didn't wait around for the creature to die. I released the lever and standing on the weakening shark's spine, I yanked out the spear. Then using the shark's body, I pushed myself upwards. My timing of ascent was crucial because of the ocean pressure.

I rose up slowly using my feet as paddles. 'Need any help brother?' and from all over the ocean appeared hundreds of dolphins. Without a word, a school of dolphins formed a platform with their sleek and powerful bodies and gently carried me up to the surface. Others formed a ring around my body protecting me. Finally, after what seemed like eternity, I saw the sunlight shining through the crystal waters above. The great dolphins gently carried me to the surface where I was immediately pulled into a boat.

The magnificent dolphins made one last show before they departed. They shot up out of the water and performed acrobatic feats of a kind that none of the people had ever seen in their lives. The people shouted with glee. Others laughed, while some cried with mirth until their sides hurt. Then as one well-drilled platoon, the impressive dolphins stood on their tails, faced the crowd and swam out to sea, one powerful and magnificent army of the sea.

'Thank you and goodbye, friends,' I whispered as I was taken to the hospital, where I recovered from my ordeal. I was told I was saved in the nick of time because a lot of tail fins swarmed the surface everywhere. They began attacking the dead white shark, tearing it to pieces.

That strange secret part of me has never been told to anyone. Even Shannan does not utter a word. She is now grown up and acts more ladylike. I now work as a scientific officer, trying to save the great white sharks of the sea. Sometimes, I can talk to the animals of the sea. But most times, I try hard to conceal the phenomenon that for some strange reason was bestowed upon me. I sense that someday I will fulfil my destiny. All the living things and I have an understanding, they leave us alone, and we let them be. We try to reinforce a world of perfect harmony.

Great stories were created and told a hundred times about the young man who had killed a great white shark, 100 metres long, and as huge as a whole playing field. After six months of aggressive campaigning, the fish waste by the KM Tuna Cannery was relocated elsewhere. People started swimming at the bay again. I still have my spear gun, hanging over my door. Sometimes, in my dreams, a chubby and pot-bellied man comes out and talks to me.

Things to do after reading

Activity 1

- Who is Jake? Is there anything special about him? What do you think about Shannan? Should she be blamed for her actions?
- Was the spear gun really magical? Describe how you can tell?
- Have you seen a great white shark? Are all sharks dangerous?
- Do you find this story has any moral values? What are the lessons to be learned here?

Activity 2

Imaginative extension

- What do you think Jake was thinking as he sped through the bush track? Do you think the animals should have told Jake what was happening? Why?
- Imagine that you have a naughty brother being attacked by a vicious crocodile or wild boar. In this case you can't kill it except by magic. Write the first paragraph or the last paragraph to the story.

Activity 3

Extended writing

Write a story about a girl with magical powers. Imagine that either she is good or evil and wants to do something good or bad to our Mama Graun. She could have the following powers:

- ability to change animals and things into different forms
- the ability to disappear and reappear in any forms
- the ability to cause changes in nature. For example, cause floods, rain and dry season, etc.

The great exodus

Beyond the blue horizon where the gentle sea appears to meet the clear Salamaua sky, I squint my eyes to see the smiling sun rising above the Bismarck Sea. I stretch my short arms and legs and welcome another new day. I feel excited. For some unknown reason, a feeling of satisfaction floods all over me. Then it suddenly dawns on me that I am on an island with Zigori. An island filled with all the wonders that I had only dreamed about. For a second, I think I am hallucinating but this is real. I am on the Island of Paradise.

Our new island home is in a place called Nambis Bay. It is a beautiful place. The blue sea is crystal clear. When the sun shines on the surface, it dazzles like opals. Pure untouched white sand surrounds the bay and every time the sun changes positions, it radiates sparking light from every direction. Trees grow right to the edge of the water and plants and shrubs dangle over the dazzling blue ocean, creating shade where fish swim in abundance. It is really a paradise island and it belonged to Zigori and myself. It was our home, our paradise.

Our days were spent attending to a number of things. We ate when we were hungry, slept, played or went about exploring the island. Sometimes when we played, we rolled and plunged ourselves into the beautiful sand. We could smell the freshness of the pure earth; it caused us to hold our breath.

We marvelled at this wonder and at this land of freedom. The feeling I got was beyond description and it brought tears to my eyes. I was happy beyond words and I often wondered how long this would last.

But whenever my feelings were down, there was always Zigori to cheer me up. He was funny, energetic and adventurous.

'Hey Titi, what are you daydreaming about, uh? You're not crying again, are you?' Zigori said grinning.

I was startled. 'Eh, what did you say?' I asked blinking my eyes. 'I must have dozed off under a coconut tree.'

'Oh nothing,' Zigori said grinning from ear to ear.

'What are you grinning about?' I asked sitting up.

'Uh, I'm sorry Titi,' he apologised. Then his round face lit up. 'Hey, can we play hide and seek?' He knew I liked that game.

'Oh, that's a great idea, Zigori.' I said getting to my feet excitedly. 'I will close my eyes and count up to ten.'

'Oh no, not again,' muttered Zigori under his breath.

'Did you say something, Zigori?' I asked pretending to be angry.

'Let's play, but you go and hide first' he said.

'No, you go and hide first. I'll try and find you!' I said, knowing he always wanted to hide first.

'Okay, that's fine! But don't spy on me, okay?' he declared putting his short arms on his chest. 'Put your little head in your shell and stay in there, until you finish counting!'

'Oh, Zigori! You're hurting my feelings. You know I don't cheat!' I said with a smile.

Zigori said nothing but waited for me to do as he'd ordered. Finally with some reluctance, I went into my shell, grunting and mumbling.

Zigori sped off and hid.

So we played and had fun. During the game, it turned out that when Zigori hid in the sand I spotted him quickly. When it was my turn it was an endless search for him to find me. I was becoming skilful at camouflaging myself in this beautiful white sandy beach. I began to enjoy myself more than Zigori. He started grumbling.

'Hey Titi, how come you are good at this hide and seek game?'

'I learned the trick from the elders, Zigori. Didn't you?'

'No, I missed that part. Please, can you teach me?'

'That's not a problem.'

And in the weeks that followed, I taught Zigori the skills of concealing oneself. Zigori did not realise this, but the skills he learned could one day save his life.

When we got tired of sunbathing and scurrying into the sand we would dive into the blue sea and have a delightful swim. One day, after lots of exploring and playing, Zigori said, 'Let's look for food. I'm famished.'

Our food was seaweeds, corals and small fish. And oh boy, food was in abundance. This was an untouched island. There were no other turtles species or larger animals like the two-legged human beings living here—just us with our children and grand children. It was a remote location, too far to reach by canoe. This suited us well. We enjoyed the freedom of having everything to ourselves. We both believed that this was a place we had been blessed with by our ancestors.

This was how our normal everyday passed. Each day we learned new tricks and taught each other survival skills.

We are of the *Chelonia mydas* tribe or, as some call us, green turtles. Our relatives live many kilometres away from here. Our isolation from our relatives was not intentional. We had been living happily with our folks and one time in the dry season of June, many moons ago, Zigori and I had ventured into the neighbouring islands and came across this gorgeous coral atoll. We found no other animals or *Chelonia mydas* living here. So we decided to make this our new home.

I recall clearly the day we decided to tell our folks our intention to leave. Our parents thought that it was weird but they did not try to stop us. In a way it was good because food was becoming scarce. Some of the children were only too happy with our decision to move. Zigori and I excelled in a number of activities and they were quite jealous of our abilities. But we didn't mind. We in fact enjoyed the challenges and the more they tried, the better we became.

'I hear Titi and Zigori are planning to move. Have you heard about that?' asked one of our friends to another turtle.

'No, I haven't. But if they are, that is good!'

'Why? Won't we miss them?' asked a friend who was from the leatherback family. They were a giant family of turtles and we had shared the island habitat for many generations. They respected our species and we did likewise.

'Nay. Let them go! We'll have more room for ourselves,' said one of the elder turtles.

They were happy we were going because it was getting kind of overcrowded. The island we called home housed many species of turtles. There were leatherback turtles, ridley turtles, green sea turtles and lots of others species. This island was unique in many aspects. On one part of the ocean the water was freezing cold, while on another location, the water was warm. Food had been plentiful, but with a large growing population, it was sometimes difficult to find food. But this had been our heaven until we left.

My father was sad but he understood. 'I will bring your issue to the clan meeting. But you will have to wait. It will be held on the next full moon!'

'That's great, Dad. Thanks for your understanding.'

He hugged me. 'Don't thank me yet. Wait until you hear from the council!'

We were informed that the meeting was to be in two weeks time and we could hardly wait. It seemed like a long time, but finally, the day arrived. All sorts of thoughts flashed before me. I said to Zigori, 'Let's pray and ask our great ancestors to release us to this new land.'

'Come, let us go over to the boulder and pray.'

So hand in hand we moved off to our sacred place of prayer.

Meanwhile, attendances for the meeting turned out well. There were turtles of all kinds. There were freshwater turtles, sea turtles and deep ocean-going turtles. This migration issue was very important and the chief had

called a meeting of all the family of turtles. My father presented the case on our behalf. After weighing up our chances of survival and maturity, we were finally given permission to depart. And gosh, it was some farewell! I recalled the sadness and the long journey to get here. But it had been worth it. We love our new home!

One day Zigori said to me. 'It is now two years since we left and nobody has visited us. What do you think has happened back home?'

I thought for a while and replied. 'Perhaps, nobody knows the way here, eh?'

'That's probably true,' murmured Zigori. 'But my instincts tell me that something terrible has happened back at home.'

I didn't want to believe that and brushed the idea aside. 'Uh, maybe they have gone to another island.'

'But somebody would have come and told us,' said Zigori thoughtfully.

'Ahiee, I know,' I said with a huge smile. 'I believe they are preparing for the sand dancing festivity that is held every June. Don't you remember?'

Zigori smiled grimly. 'Yes, that could be it, but-but—

'Not buts, Zigori,' I said firmly.

He frowned in deep thought. Something was not right. Yes, he did recall that this was a special time of the year, when all the turtles that lived on the land, in the shallow and deep waters, come together to dance and lay eggs. 'Yeah, I remember the time!' he thought with much happiness.

But something still troubled his thoughts.

'Well that could be true, Titi,' he finally muttered.

But I saw that Zigori was still troubled. 'If you are worried, how about paying them a visit, eh? You could invite them to our island!' I suggested with a smile. I was missing my friends too and wanted to know what was happening in our old home.

Zigori nodded his head in confirmation. 'That is a good idea, Titi! I think I'll pay them a visit. You take care of our children and remain here, please!'

'Yes, I agree! I'll mind home while you go. It's better to know what's happening than to be left in the dark.'

That night I dreamed terrible dreams. I woke up screaming in the night.

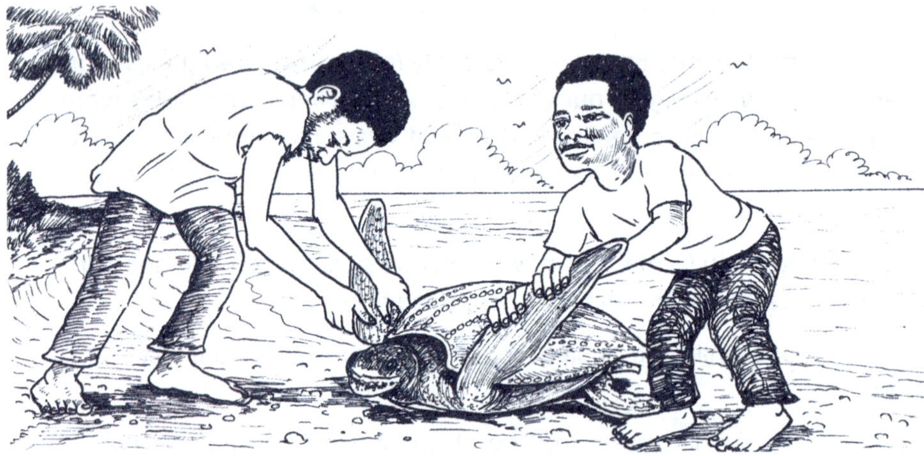

'Titi? Titi, what's wrong?' Zigori asked pounding on my back.

'Uh, I don't know,' I said crawling out of my shell. 'I had this terrible dream. The two-legged humans were chasing our friends. I was caught—uh!' I began to weep quietly. 'Oh, Zigori, it was horrible!'

'Shsssh, go to sleep sweetheart! It was only a dream!' he said as he hugged me. His strong arms gave me comfort and I fell into a deep sleep. When I woke the next morning, the sun was already up. I yawned and stretched out, rolling in the clear white sand.

'Now, are you awake?' Zigori asked with a grin. I nodded my head. 'That's good, sleepy head!' he said with much love.

It was time for him to go. I noticed that for some strange reason, the sea lay motionless as the early morning sun peeked out of the placid skies. We stood around and Zigori bid the children and me farewell. We watched him as he swam away, heading North to the waters of the Makassar Strait. You see we have very good memories. We always know where we were born and go back there to lay our eggs. We turtles have a sixth sense for finding our homes.

The distance between our new home and our former habitat was quite far. From Nambis Bay, Zigori was going to swim through the Bismarck Sea, then enter the Makassar Strait, through Celebes Islands and finally land on the small Island of Laut. It was a long journey that Zigori was going to make. He would go through rough seas, shark-infested waters and pass fishing vessels that travelled between the Straits. But these thoughts did not deter him. It only fuelled his determination to go to his friends.

Once in the deep ocean, Zigori swam easily, not bothering to take a break. Even though he had short legs, his flippers helped a lot. He swam beneath the water and then regularly surfaced to draw air into his lungs. He swam tirelessly for two whole days. At the end of the third day, he felt tired. He was getting old.

Zigori thought back to a couple of years earlier. He was stronger then and would have enjoyed the challenge. But now he was tiring. In the distance he could see the sun setting rapidly over the Blue Mountains, its receding rays casting yellow golden rays over the blue ocean. If he were not tired, he would have loved to watch the golden sunset. But he needed to find a spot to rest. He reached the island and slept under a crop of rocks.
It was safe enough. He whispered to himself, 'I will continue the trip again tomorrow at first light. I am sure I will arrive in the afternoon when everybody is getting ready for dinner. I am sure to get a good reception.'

Dreaming about the reception, he fell fast asleep. Before long he snored into the cold eerie night, dreaming about two-legged humans trying to catch him. Half the night he woke up to strange noises and by early morning light, although feeling tired, Zigori took off on his journey.

He scooted into the water in great haste, lifting his head to the surface once in a while for fresh air, then on again. The miles went by. Suddenly, in the distance he could see his old village. He found renewed strength and swam rapidly, until he saw the land of his birth, about a kilometre away. He knew he was home. The desire to reunite with his family and clan was burning like a fire inside him.

Zigori reached the beach just as the sun stood on top of Mt Celebes, displaying its awesome red, yellow and gold, then a last flash of light, before it sank into nothingness. Zigori stepped gingerly on to the greyish white sand he knew so well. The nostalgia of being home was real. A happy tear rolled down his cheeks, which Zigori removed in a hurry. Then grinning with happiness, Zigori rolled on the sand and jumped up and down with great exhilaration. He had finally made it and all alone!

But he felt awkward. He looked about him. 'Am I in the right place?' he asked himself with concern. He soon realised that there was nobody around to give him the warm welcome he had anticipated. He was puzzled and a little unsettled. 'Hey, is anybody home? Hello,' he called out softly.

He got no immediate reply. The howling wind blowing through the Makassar Strait and the continuous smashing of the waves against the reefs at the shore were the only sounds he heard. Feeling weird but not intimidated, Zigori called out again, louder this time. 'It's me, Zigori! I have come for a visit! Is anybody home?' Still there was no answer. There was no sign of anyone, not even the seagulls that graced the beautiful white sands. He examined the beach and saw no sign of any turtle's feet. That's strange. He heard the silent rustle of the leaves and the howling of the wind against the cliff edges. He felt the vibrations of the earth shake when the waves rolled and smashed against the rocks and boulders near the sea. An eerie feeling began to creep all over him.

'I am sure that, this is my place of birth,' he told himself firmly. Feeling lost but sure that he had come to the right place, Zigori sat down on a boulder. A smile crept to his lips as he saw the boulder he had unconsciously selected to sit on. We had often sat on the same boulder. 'Thanks for reminding me, I'm home,' he said as he patted the rock. He waited sensing that there was a reason for everything.

Suddenly he heard some scratching noises behind him. Followed by other more pronounced grunting noises. 'Oh, they are here,' he whispered. 'I have come home!' The feeling of happiness threatened to engulf him. Zigori held his breath and waited patiently. From the corner of his eyes, he saw his friends coming out of their hideouts one by one. Some swam ashore, others emerged out of the sand, while many more came out from under various boulders.

'Zigori? Is that you, Zigori?' one turtle asked anxiously as he came forward boldly.

'Yes, it's Zigori,' said a dwarf turtle appearing from the side of the boulder Zigori was sitting upon.

'Zigori! Zigori is really here!' and he heard his name being relayed all over.

Turtles ran towards him shouting and chanting their welcome songs. They hugged and pushed him around in great happiness and danced on the beach. The dancing went all night and into the daylight hours. The chief had to step in and stop the dancing and feasting. 'Take a break fellows. Tomorrow we will talk!'

Zigori's father was still alive and he was very happy. 'Son, come let's go to bed. You can tell us all about your home tomorrow!' And with arms wrapped tightly around each other, they moved off.

'Thanks, Dad,' Zigori whispered huskily. His dad tightened his arms fiercely around Zigori to let him know that he was happy that Zigori had come back. That night, or what was left of it, was the best sleep Zigori could recall ever having. 'Well, not really but close!' he thought with a smile.

The next day, the cool Celebes breeze was blowing over the island cooling the hot turtles. All the tribes of turtles were present. But for some strange reason, Zigori did not see as many turtles as he thought there would be. He was shocked and sat in silence.

The chief cleared his throat and stood up. 'Zigori, my son, we are so relieved to see you are alive. We thought we would never see you again!' he paused smiling. 'Look, you've grown some and I am sure, become wiser too.'

'And brave too to visit us across this dangerous sea,' said a leatherback turtle with respect. He was as old as time. His ancestors lived as far back as the Cretaceous Period—that's 100 million years ago when the dinosaurs still existed. Zigori had heard stories told by the leatherbacks that their prehistoric ancestors had witnessed the fall of dinosaurs and the rise of humanity.

'We believe Titi is in good health, uh?' the chief asked raising his eyebrows.

'She's fine and send her greetings to you all, friends,' Zigori said with pride. 'The children also send their greetings!'

'Oh, you have children too. How many— uh?' he asked hesitantly.

'We have 50 children and over 300 grand children.'

'Uh, that many—?' and there was whistles and cheering.

The chief stepped in quickly. 'That's great Zigori. May your years of living be doubled in your new home!'

'Thanks Chief! But, please tell me about yourself,' and Zigori gestured with his short hands. 'I don't see so many, sir?'

The chief moved over and sat next to Zigori on the boulder. He began to tell his story. 'Since Titi and you left, we have been attacked by the two-legged monsters on our island quite a number of times. Each time they come, our numbers dwindle. They come in canoes with spears and capture many of our species. Just last month, they captured six of our children and took them away. It is now two weeks since their departure!'

Zigori heard soft weeping coming from one mother and he felt a terrible rage built up inside him. 'Have you tried to run away?' he asked, knowing it was a silly question.

'Where to, Zigori? Where to—?' the chief said with much sadness.

My father said, 'We are quite scared that the missing children will not return, just like the others. And I know that these humans will appear again!'

'Oh, that's why they were in hiding,' Zigori thought sadly.

The chief confirmed it. 'That is why we were hiding when you showed up. It is not like the good old days. We used to play and spend endless hours looking for food and sunbathing on this very boulder. We live in fear of the two-legged man. They are relentless and I know they will come to capture us again!'

Zigori understood. As he imagined more about these humans, he shuddered with fear.

'Zigori, why don't you tell us something about your home?'

'Yes, please do!' said my father.

'Oh please, do tell us about your new home, friend,' one of the leatherback turtles said.

Zigori cleared his throat and began. 'Our new home is beautiful with lots of food to eat. It is an isolated location, difficult for boats to get to. Even if they did, the wind in the strait is fairly rough and can overturn any small vessel. Sharks are plentiful and they are not friendly. Although they rarely attack us.' Everyone sat in rapt silence listening, as he told the tribe about our new paradise.

'Friends, I am much grieved to hear that this island is no longer safe for you. May the gods of our ancestors prevent the humans from coming again.'

'We have been praying for that too!' said the chief sadly.

Zigori stood up and slid down the boulder he had been sharing with the chief. 'Friends, I'd like to make an announcement, please!'

The turtles stopped whatever they were doing and all eyes focused on Zigori. 'If you feel threatened and decide to search for a new home, I'd like to say that all of you are welcome to our island. You can make Nambis Bay your new home!' And then he sat down.

No one moved, or said anything. It was so quiet you could hear a pin drop. Everyone sat silently digesting the invitation. At last the chief volunteered, 'Uh, thanks for your invitation, Zigori. We really appreciate that kind offer!'

Zigori whispered, 'My home is your home. You all are welcome.' Everybody clapped and cheered.

Many of the turtles stood up and thanked Zigori. 'Thank you! Thank you!' said the giant leatherback turtle. Everybody now felt there was some light, at the end of the dark tunnel. When Zigori finished his short speech, the chief stood up. 'Thank you Zigori! We will keep your offer in our minds. At least there is a place to settle, if we feel unsafe here. For now, we will wait for the lost ones! Where there is hope, there is life!'

Everybody murmured, 'Yes! Yes the two leatherbacks and four green turtles captured might come back home.'

The meeting ended around mid-afternoon and everybody departed to look for food. In the evening they burrowed into the earth and slept but the smell of fear hung in the air like a bad odour. Zigori found it difficult to sleep. He tossed and turned all night.

Zigori awoke early the next morning feeling tired. He stretched his flippers and after a dive in the ocean he felt much better. He went and spoke to his father. 'I will have to return to my family. They will be worried. I only came for a visit, Dad. Now that I know you are safe, I have got to go back father!'

The old turtle replied, 'Zigori my son. You have a family to care for. They need you more than we do! Thank you for the visit and when you return pass our best wishes and may they all live many long years!'

The chief came over when he heard that Zigori was intending to leave. 'Zigori, your visit has added more life and courage to our people. Many thanks for your help and of course, not forgetting your invitation.'

'I have given you the directions, sir. Should you want to come, we will be glad to have you.' Then Zigori moved around shaking everyone's hands. When that was done, he moved to the shores. The turtles all assembled along the shores and watched, some waved. Others cried gently.

'Good-bye everyone,' called Zigori as he took a plunge into the sea. Within minutes he was out of sight.

Back in the land of Zigori's birth, life was normal again. For a full year the turtles lived peacefully and bred plenty of young ones. So one day, the chief said to his people. 'I think the two-legged creatures will not return! They have taken many of our friends and I believe they think we have fled our homes. The Gods of our ancestors must have struck them down.' Everybody was happy for a time believing their wise old chief's reasoning. Until unexpectedly one terrible day, the two-legged monsters returned to their home. There were six of them in two boats. The warning was sounded but too late. The men chased the turtles, looking for the largest ones. This gave time for many of the young ones to escape into the sea. But forty turtles were caught. The humans bundled the turtles up and took them away, never to be seen again.

On the shores of the old island, the turtles wailed and grieved for their captured friends and loved ones. Toi, a playmate of the kidnapped friends, moaned and said, 'If I were their size and strength, I could chase after and rescue my friends. I am helpless!'

'My God! My God! What can I do?' wept another leatherback turtle.

Another wept bitterly. 'Am I a coward? I can face sharks in the sea with no fright but I can't fight these monsters. The spirit of my ancestors, please help me.'

'Oh, ho-o-oo. What can I do?' cried one female turtle.

When the chief heard the cries of his people he could take it no more. 'I want all of you to get ready. At dawn, you will swim across this vast sea to Nambis Bay. It will be a safe home for you. There you can live freely in peace!'

A young turtle asked, 'I don't know why these two-legged men hunt us down. We never hurt them. We never destroy their homes. I wish they could leave us alone! But, they don't! They keep on coming again and again. Not long we will all disappear!'

Every turtle wept miserably for his or her lost friend.

'I don't want to go!' stifled one mother greenback turtle. 'This has been my home for generations!' Many were concerned about the idea of losing their beautiful island home. It was too much to tolerate.

The chief felt the heartaches of his people and he bled for them. There was nothing he could do. He knew that once word got around to other humans of their locations, many would come running. He immediately called up the eldest in the clan for an urgent meeting. They all gathered around the chief, each dreading but sensing what he had decided.

'Fellow comrades,' the chief said calmly. 'For years and years, we have lived on this island of our great forefathers. We have never heard nor experienced such tragedy. But the situation is clear, I don't need to explain myself!' he paused, feeling sad for taking such a stand. 'We will take Zigori's advice and move to the new island to live with him. Perhaps, there will be peace there?'

No one made any sound. The elders just stood or sat silently rocking to and fro in deep thought. 'I can't force you to go! But if you don't—' he left the sentence unfinished.

When no one volunteered a comment he went on. 'Personally speaking, and I am only speaking for myself, I think I will stay while the rest of you go! My roots are buried here—' and the noble head, the chief who was the oldest of all the turtles bowed his head. The other turtles sensed his discomfort and were silent. In a broken voice, the chief declared, 'This is where my great ancestors lived and are buried here. I will die here!'

Slowly but surely, turtles started clapping. First one, then two, three and finally all the elders clapped and cheered. The leader stood in front of his elders, tears streaming down his wrinkled old cheeks. He tried to say something, but he could not. A lump caught in his throat. He made no attempt to wipe the tears; he let them flow freely.

Zigori's father stood up. 'Chief, we will follow you to the ends of the earth, sir! If you stay, I stay too!'

Another turtle added, 'I don't want to go. I will stay with you and die here!'

'Yes, I will stay here too! This is where I was born and raised up,' said an elderly turtle. 'Perhaps, this is the time!'

Not a single turtle that was in the group was less than 50 years old. The chief was rumoured to be around 500 years plus, but no one really knew his age. All the turtles in the council of elders voted to stay back. Not one had second thoughts. 'Well friends, thanks a lot! If this is how you feel then we will let the young ones know. They have to go to safeguard the future generations of our kind!'

'That's right friends,' said Zigori's father. 'If we don't do that we will become extinct. The two-legged men are capturing us for their selfish needs. On the other end, if we all go, these monsters might get suspicious. Then they will search for us into the new land. Let some of us remain. We have lived long enough!'

There was general agreement all around.

In the evening, they broke the news to the other turtles. There was much crying and sadness on the island. A feast was thrown. It was a day and night of rejoicing and heartbreak. Everybody was saddened but this was the great circle of life. This exodus was for freedom to breed, and freedom to live for them and the next generation yet to come. Each turtle hugged their elders and with heavy hearts dived into the sea, early the next morning. If someone had counted, they would have counted well over five thousand of the last remaining, leatherbacks and *Chelonia mydas* of the Pacific, making an exodus to a new home, a new land. To this day, no one has ever found out what happened to the missing turtles, nor have they found the Island of Zigori.

Things to do after reading

Activity 1

Write your own story after reading this tale. It can be a factual story about a natural phenomenon you have seen, heard or read about. You can weave it into a poem, a tale like this or record your story verbally using a tape recorder.

Activity 2

What do you think of this story? Is it trying to teach us something? Often many tales have a moral message. Does this story? Look at passages of the story to back up what you are saying.

Activity 3

Examine the creativity of the passage and the way the words describe situations. While English is not our mother tongue, we do have the ability to put our thoughts into words. What is the intention of this author? Who is he or she trying to reach?

Report

Facts about sea turtles

About sea turtles

Sea turtles are some of the largest turtles in the world and they live in almost every ocean, including our very own waters in Papua New Guinea.

How do sea turtles protect themselves?

Sea turtles protect themselves from predators with their shells, large size, and thick scaly skin on their heads and necks, but they are not able to pull their heads into their shells.

How long do they live for?

Most sea turtles live approximately 15 to 20 years and may live to be 80 years old.

What do sea turtles look like?

They have smooth shells and paddle-like flippers, which help to glide through the water as fast as 24 kilometres an hour. They are able to swim long distances. For example, the Loggerhead turtles migrate over 12 000 km across the Pacific.

What do sea turtles eat?

They eat jellyfish, seaweed, crabs, shrimp, snails, algae and molluscs.

Adult sea turtles

Every 2 to 3 years, it is time for female sea turtles to lay their eggs on the beach. They leave the ocean at night: they are slow and defenceless on the land. It can take between one and three hours to nest. The female turtle will lay 50–200 eggs in the nest, covers them up with sand so that the eggs are hidden and then returns to the sea. Male sea turtles almost never leave the water.

Baby sea turtles (hatchlings)

Baby turtles are called hatchlings and they come out of their eggs after about two months. The hatchlings come out at night and make their way to the water. It is a dangerous journey and predators wait to eat them. When it is time for these turtles to lay eggs, it is believed that they return to where they themselves hatched.

The seven sea turtle species

There are seven species of sea turtles: Australia flatback, Green, Hawksbill, Kemp's ridley, Leatherback, Loggerhead, and Olive ridley. They are all protected, which means you are not allowed to kill or capture them.

AUSTRALIAN FLATBACK

- medium-sized
- nest on beaches in unpopulated areas of the northern coast of Australia
- saltwater crocodiles, as well as monitor lizards and foxes, sometimes eat small adult turtles while they are nesting

GREEN

- medium-to-large sea turtle
- gets its name from the green colour of its body fat
- eats turtle grass and other marine plants

HAWKSBILL

- medium-sized sea turtle
- found in tropical waters around the world
- named for its birdlike beak
- mates in shallow water off the nesting beach
- climb over reefs and rocks to nest among the roots of vegetation on beaches near its feeding grounds

KEMP'S RIDLEY

- also called the Atlantic ridley
- the world's most endangered sea turtle
- in 1947, over forty thousand female Kemp's ridley turtles nested on that beach in a single day; in 1992, only five hundred came to nest. Because they come in numbers to lay their eggs, poachers find them easy prey.

LEATHERBACK

- the largest of all sea turtles—can grow to over 2 metres long, and weigh up to 200 kilograms
- can dive to great depths, as far as 914 metres, probably in search of their favourite food: jellyfish.

LOGGERHEAD

- known for its massive reddish brown head
- eats fish, jellyfish, mussels, clams, squid, shrimp, seaweed, and marine grasses
- travels widely and has been found as far as 805 kilometres offshore
- in many areas of the world, this turtle is hunted for its meat and eggs.

OLIVE RIDLEY

- also called the Pacific ridley
- this small sea turtle has paddle-like flippers and grows up to 71 centimetres long
- a speedy nester, it spends only about forty-five minutes on the beach laying its eggs

You would notice with interest that none of these reptiles eat human flesh. If they don't eat us, why do we hunt them down? Just think about it. These huge creatures are clumsy on the land and work very hard to lay their eggs. I am sure they are not capable of hurting a fly. Please, please, we must try to protect these gentle creatures. In order to do that, we must stop buying any products dealing with turtle. This will at least help.

The Legend of Kauila at Punalu'u

Long, long ago, a magnificent turtle appeared on the moonlit shores of Punalu'u. Honu-po'o-kea was no ordinary sea turtle. Her head was as white as the snows of Mauna Kea. Honu-po'o-kea paused at the ocean's edge, searching for the perfect place to build a nest. Gentle waves tugged at the black sand beneath her. With a deep sigh, she pulled herself ashore.

Honu-po'o-kea dug a shallow hole and laid an egg, as dark and smooth as polished kauila wood. Her mate, Honu-'ea, had been waiting offshore, his reddish-brown shell bobbing in the surf. As Honu-po'o-kea covered her nest, Honu-'ea joined her. Together the turtles dug into the black sand and created a spring. Then, as silently as they had come, they disappeared into the ocean.

In time, the egg hatched into a magical turtle named Kauila. Kauila made her home at the bottom of the freshwater spring that her parents had made. People called it Ka wai hu o Kauila, the rising water of Kauila. Children would come to play in the spring, and if they saw bubbles rising from its depths they knew that Kauila was sleeping. Sometimes Kauila would transform herself into a girl so that she could play among the keiki. Always, she kept a watchful eye on the children, ensuring their safety.

Honu, or green sea turtles, still come to the black sands of Punalu'u on the Big Island. They can be seen grazing on seaweed in the surf or basking in the warm sun, oblivious to the people that gather to watch them. At night the rare honu 'ea, or hawksbill turtle, has been known to nest in the area, just as Honu-po'o-kea did so long ago.

Here and there the black sand bubbles as cool mountain water from Mauna Loa percolates through the porous lava. This was Kauila's gift: fresh water for the people of Punalu'u. Long ago Hawaiians would dive to the floor of the bay to collect the fresh water in gourds. Hence, the name Punalu'u means, Diving Spring.

Things to do after reading

If you are connected to the Internet, browse and find out more information about the turtle species. The class teacher could set an assignment or research paper.

Activity 1

Look at pictures of turtles in a book and write a story about one of the turtles. Get this story corrected by your teacher and then send it in to the newspapers.

Activity 2

Investigate the market place with your teacher and educate the people about the endangered species of turtles. Let them know that there are laws to protect the turtles.

Activity 3

Write to the Minister for Environment and Conversation asking for a law to protect an island or area near your home or in PNG. Get help from an organisation like WWF South Pacific for your project.

Procedure 4

Could fires have come from volcanoes in Papua New Guinea?

Nambis and Mambis were best mates. They were in grade 6 and attended the Solowara Primary School at Limanda. Both were renowned for the great stories they told. One day, during lunchtime, Mambis gathered all the children in his class together and proceeded to tell them this story.

'Boys and girls, do you know how fire came to the Highlands?' he asked the children.

'Oh no, we don't know how fire came to the Highlands. Oh, please tell us—' the children all chorused.

'Great, I'll be pleased to tell you the anecdote. But please children, pay attention?' he asked with mock seriousness. The children all pretended to be grave. They loved Mambis and Nambis because of the wonderful traditional legends they took turns in telling. Now it was Mambis's turn and they were ready.

'A long time ago there was no fire in the Highlands of Papua New Guinea. In those far-off days, a man and his wife lived with their sons near a place called Waimress in the Chimbu district. They lived there all their lives and they had never seen or heard of fires.

'One day a wily white-tail bird flew by and sat on a casuarina tree, which grew in front of the man's kunai hut. The man and his family lived in this hut with a young pig and a dog that the man had tamed years ago. The bird flew about performing its usually chirping and dancing displays trying to wake up the man who was snoring loudly under the tree. As it flew about from branch to branch, one of the seeds from the casuarina tree fell down and entered the man's nostrils, blocking his air passage. The man woke up with a start, cursing. As he rubbed his nostrils angrily he saw movements in the tree and knew who was the cause of his discomfort. 'Naughty bird.' He sneezed trying to blow out the casuarina nut lodged deep within his nasal cavity.

'Serves him right for sleeping under the tree,' said one of the children under his breath.

'Shsssh, keep quiet!' hissed Tupenny, the class captain.

Mambis took no notice. He continued with the story, his brown eyes twinkling and his voice taking on a deep hypnotising voice. The children knew this rhythm and they sat still, eyes open with wonder. This was the magical part—the chanting of the different characters' voices and varying the voices to express each event as if it were really happening. For Mambis was a great storyteller and he loved telling the tales this way.

'As he sat up, the bird's beautiful voice chirped this song.

"Way down where the sky meets the earth,
A mountain is weeping red, yellow and orange tears,
Tears hot enough to send a growing tree to dust,
And sending huge clouds higher than any bird can fly over.
The glowing tears eat up the trees and smoulder the animals,
Changing them to dust.
It is terrible.
No animal is safe,
No vegetation is safe.
Even the waters foam angrily,
Sending vapour-like clouds shooting miles into the sky.
We run for our lives,
But the huts glow with the same colour red and yellow,
Sending the foul-smelling odour of burnt meat.
Is this what they call fire?"

'The man listened attentively while blowing the annoying casuarina nut out of his nostrils and wondered about the song.

'The man wondered, what was this thing that was called a fire? He knew what to do. He must investigate this mountain that wept red, yellow and orange tears and the huts that glowed at night. He called his pet pig over and instructed him to journey into the unknown land where the water meets the sky. "See if you can bring me the tears that glow—fire."

'The pig wandered off into the jungle and travelled with the aid of the wily white tail to find this thing called fire. The man waited for two months and at last he saw the pig coming back limping. A close examination revealed that one of the pig's forelegs was horribly sore.'

By this time the children were all mesmerised and sat in rapt silence listening to each expression. The storyteller's voice took on an even deeper tone of intonation, emphasising each word and phrase. The children hearing the story either giggled or wept openly when the tale came to the part about the pig. Mambis's voice was such that he evoked in the children a sense of unfairness and sadness that only a master storyteller can.

'Poor pig,' said Fay and tears rolled down her chubby cheeks. She did not attempt to wipe her tears.

'Oh, don't be silly. It's only a story,' said Baur with a grin.

'Shsssh, please be quiet,' said Tupenny again.

'Uh, what did he do next?' asked one of the children.

Mambis continued ignoring the questions. He knew the story would answer their questions. 'So the man called the dog next and said to him. "My friend, you must try and find me this wonderful fire and bring it to me. I know you can!"

'The dog ran off into the bush taking the same path travelled by his friend the pig.

"The poor pig didn't listen to me and lost a foot. You must follow my instructions and you will serve your master well," advised wily white tail, swooping down and riding on the dog's back.

There were smiles everywhere as the children thought about the bird and the dog becoming friends to reach a common goal. Mambis put more expression in his voice and the children sat listening to every word.

'"Oh my friend. What is this thing that weeps tears of a thousand colours? And how can I serve my master?" asked the dog.

'"The weeping tears are from a mountain that has opened its mouth and sends out red, yellow and orange hot tears, from deep within its bowl. You don't need to go there. The pig disobeyed and paid for it. Just do as I tell you friend," warned the bird.

'The dog listened carefully. "Yeah, I will do as instructed," said the dog and disappeared into the jungle. Remembering the bird's warning, the dog selected her journey and mapped out the way she would come home to her master.'

'Did she find what he was looking for?' asked the class teacher, who had come up and stood quietly listening to Mambis telling the story. He always listened to the great yarns told by Mambis and Nambis.

'Well sir, as the story goes, it took her a month to find the wonderful fire and after observing the weeping mountain and the glowing village huts, the dog stole a burning stick from a hut and raced into the jungle. As soon as the dog reached the jungle, it followed exactly the instruction given by her bird friend—wily white tail.'

'What is this weeping mountain, Nambis?' asked Shasha.

'It's the fire,' said Morris.

'No, it's not,' said Jade. 'I think the weeping—'

'Don't!' warned Tupenny again. 'Let the children come to their own conclusion. If you tell them, the story won't be interesting, uh?'

'Yeah, Tupenny's right. Go on, Mambis, tell us the rest of the story,' the teacher encouraged.

'Thanks sir,' said Mambis. 'Well, it took the dog much longer to reach her home but when she did, the man saw the dog running down the mountainside, with a big grey cloud following her. The dog seemed to be holding the end of the cloud in her mouth and pulling the rest of it behind her.

'As the dog came closer the man watched in awe. Finally, the dog ran up to her master and dropped what she was holding in her mouth. The man saw that the clouds were coming from a bundle of sticks, which had something red and glowing at the end of them. The man eagerly picked up the bundle of sticks and immediately dropped them, shaking his hand.

'"Oh? This was what they called the fire, uh, isn't it?" he asked the dog, still rubbing his burnt hand. The dog wagged her tail and showed the man how to hold the sticks. The man thanked his friend and picked up the bundle of sticks and carried it carefully into his house.

'In the house, the dog again showed the man how to light the fire by wagging her tail vigorously over the smoking charcoal. The whirling tail sent oxygen into the charcoal and soon flames shot up from the bundle. The man understood and quickly learnt. He picked up some sticks and set them over the flames. Soon smoke was curling up from his house. The people in the valley came and saw the fire and soon they had their own fire going. That was how fire spread all over the Highlands region.'

The teacher grinned as he thought about the story. Just yesterday, he had been teaching the children about the formation of volcanoes and the destruction they caused. If Mambis could make up tales like that, he had a gift. 'I must get the children to write and record the legends they hear,' he figured, smiling as he moved to his classroom.

The traditional Highlands method of starting a fire

How to start a traditional Highlands fire

You will need to collect the following:

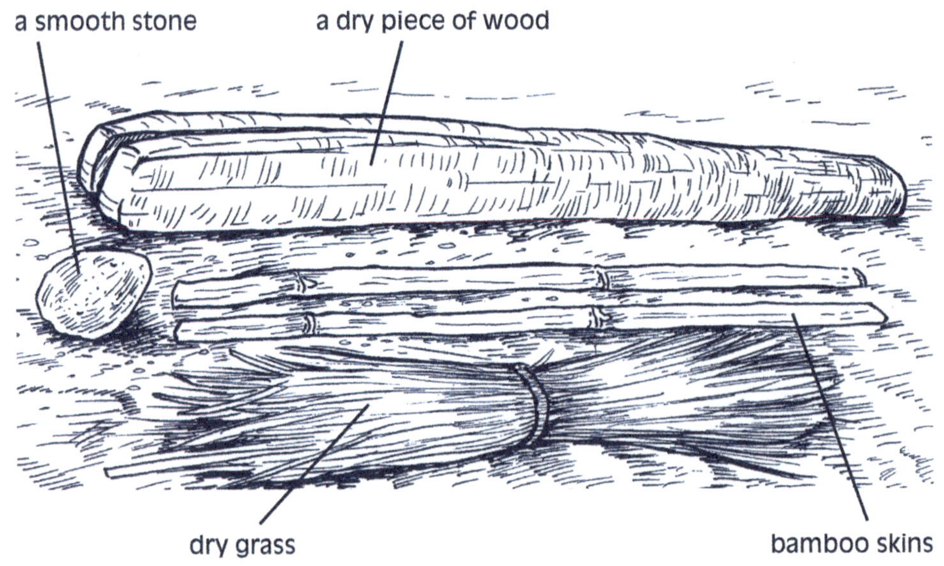

Ten steps to start a traditional fire

Follow these 10 steps accurately and soon you will have a fire burning!

Step 1: Place your dry grass in a mounded heap. A flat surface on the ground is recommended. Then in the centre of the mound where you are going to put the split wood, roll and squeeze some of the very fine dry grass.

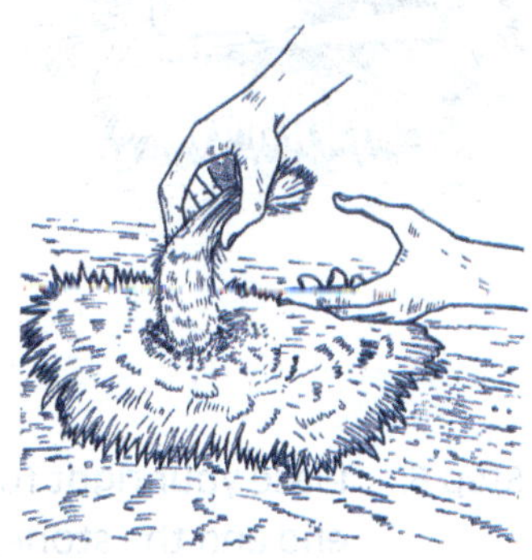

Step 2: Pick up the wood with the split end and gently place the split gap on top of the dried grass. Put a small stone between the split to create a gap. This gap is like an air passage and, with the friction, will help light the fire.

Step 3: Work out where the bamboo needs to go before you slide it under the wood. The inner part of the bamboo must touch the wood. The bamboo skin must be placed under the split gap between the stone and the unsplit end of the wood, touching the dried grass. The ends of bamboo skin must be even on both sides.

Step 4: Before moving on to the next steps, check to make sure that your set-up is correct.

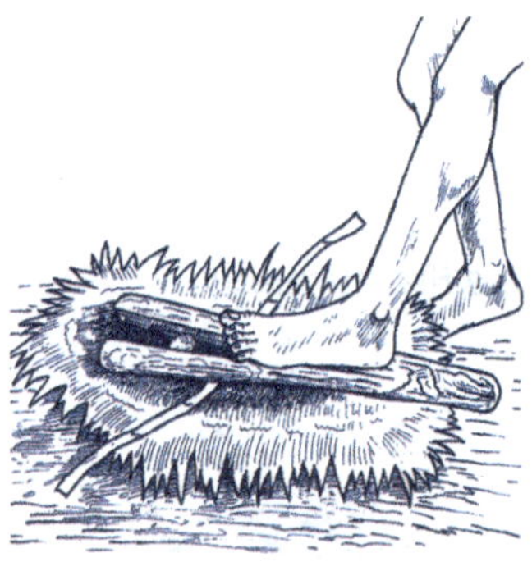

Step 5: Place your left foot on the unsplit end of the wood, making sure you do not disturb the dried grass and bamboo skin.

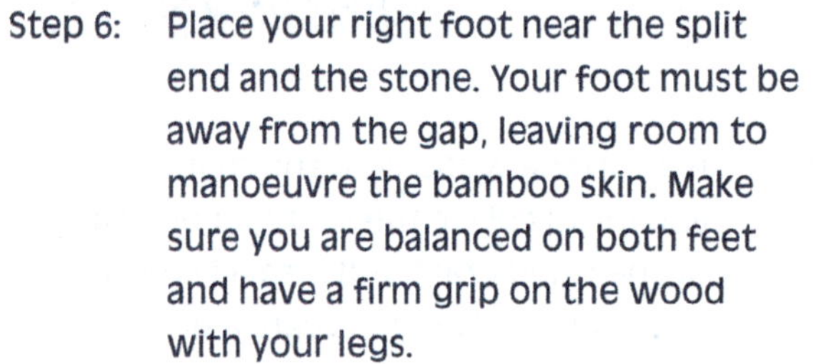

Step 6: Place your right foot near the split end and the stone. Your foot must be away from the gap, leaving room to manoeuvre the bamboo skin. Make sure you are balanced on both feet and have a firm grip on the wood with your legs.

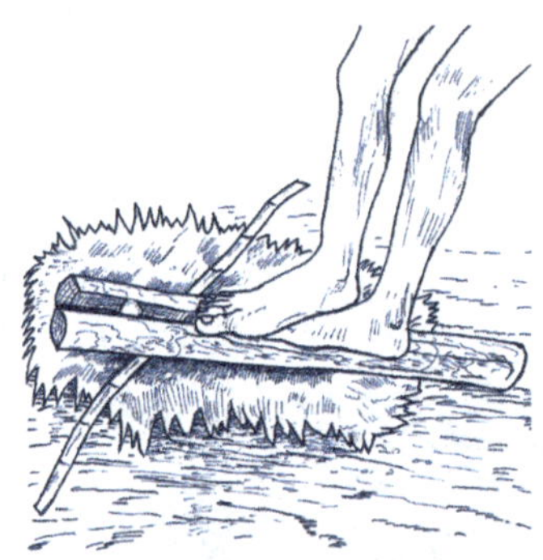

Step 7: Pick up the ends of the bamboo with your hands. For better grip, it is advisable that you twist the top end of the bamboo skins around your hands.

Step 8: Press firmly down with your legs but not too hard, so the bamboo skin can still slide forwards and backwards. For better results, place a piece of wood or branch no bigger than your toe under the split-end of the wood to elevate it a bit. This will allow for smoother operations. Then slowly pull the bamboo skin, first one way and then the other way, like two people having a tug-of-war. As soon as you develop a rhythm, you can increase your speed.

With the gradual build up in your speed, smoke will start to rise. But do not panic or hurry—just keep on pulling faster and faster until a flame erupts or your bamboo skin breaks. (Sometimes, if your bamboo skin is too thin, you will need to use two skins. Experience will teach you if this is needed.)

Step 9: When either a flame or huge smoke erupts, quickly stop and pick up the mould of grass together with the stick. Blow gently on the sparks that are causing the smoke and in no time you will have a roaring fire.

Step 10: Don't forget to collect your wood and bamboo skins, and tie them up neatly for another day.

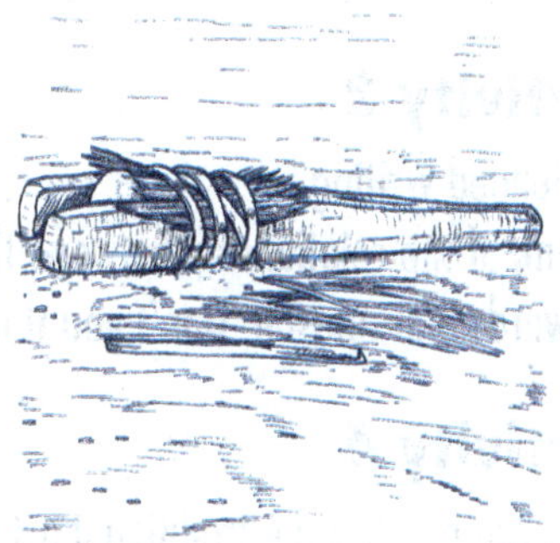

These are the 10 steps of lighting a fire using the traditional method. We should practise these methods in schools when we can, so that children can learn and retain the traditional ways of making a fire.

Things to do after reading

Activity 1

- What sort of a person is Mambis? Find some appropriate adjectives, and support your point of view with evidence from the story.
- The teacher has reached a revelation. How can his idea be accommodated in the classroom?
- Could fires have really come from volcanoes? Support your views with other evidence from your own experiences and lessons that you have learned about volcanoes or how fire began in your own area.

Activity 2

Imaginative extension

- Think about the mountain weeping tears of orange, red and yellow. Now create a poem about the texts. Read the Manam Island poem on page 108 to guide you.
- Using your imagination, show how the dog was able to bring the fire to her master. You can draw pictures to help you illustrate your work.

Activity 3

Extended Writing

Think of the relationship between the three animal friends. They must have tremendous loyalty towards their master. Don't you think? Write a story from their point of view.

Activity 4

You can practise the traditional art of making a fire.

Explanation

5

Asimba and the oak trunk

'Manam paia! Manam i paia!'

The cry shattered the peaceful night.

Within a few minutes the call went out in the village, 'Manam has erupted. Manam has finally blown up!'

The shout's echo rocketed through the dark of night, sending cold shivers into the hearts of the many inhabitants on Manam Island. Sleepers in the village heard the cry and went out to witness the spectacle. The feeling of panic was just beneath the surface, ready to blow like the volcano itself.

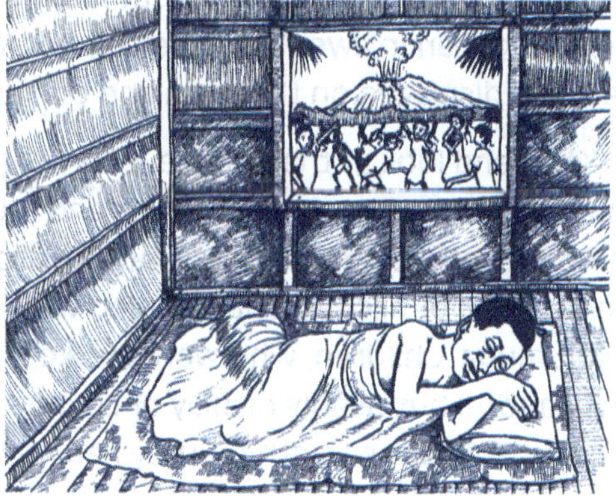

I was fast asleep, curled up on the floor, with no clue as to what was happening around me. In fact, I was in another world. I was out hunting the megapode bird's eggs I had discovered quite unexpectedly, at the foot of a giant oak tree protruding from the side of Mt Manam.

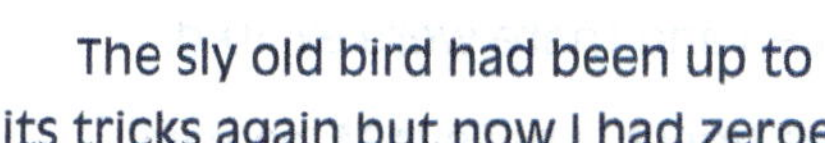

The sly old bird had been up to its tricks again but now I had zeroed in on its nest. I crept slowly towards the old tree trunk and, friends believe me, this was one old and massive tree trunk. I remember one day when 10 of us children linked our hands together and wrapped them around the trunk but we could hardly complete the task. Tales were told in the village that the massive oak trunk had magical powers but no one believed it. The legends told of generations ago when the old Oak tree had once saved the lives of the people of the island. With such superstitious beliefs, the people left the Oak alone and never touched it for firewood or such. I didn't believe such a fairy tale. I was here for a different reason. I crept closer, moving silently, anticipating my victory.

In the village, people lit kerosene lamps, torches and bomboms and began to move around uneasily. Fearful but uncertain, not knowing what to do or where to go. They could see in the distance the red, yellow and orange glows spurting sky high and causing brilliant assorted colours on Manam. 'Hey, this must be the big one the vulcanologists have been warning us about?' said one villager. 'I think we need to get ready. We may have to evacuate the island!'

'Hey look? The lava spurting out from the crater is huge!' exclaimed one young man in awe. Truly, the red-hot lava spurting out looked like the fireworks displayed on the mainland on September 16.

'Yeah, and look at that smoke. Lucky the wind is blowing out to sea or we would be covered in ashes. The volcano must have blown during the night,' stated the local priest who was moving around the village trying to calm people. Cries of excitement, mingled with fear, were heard all over the village of Kulumuga. Children, who were awake, cried excitedly as they witnessed the beautiful but deadly display of colours and gases that reached up into the heavens. This was something they had never seen and there were excited.

'We have to move and quickly,' prompted the priest. 'I believe Manam will erupt with a bigger bang!'

'Yes, I believe you are right. Call everyone to our Kibung house. We'll decide what to do,' said the village councillor. A call was sounded using the ancient cone shell, used only for emergency meetings. People responded immediately. They came, young and old alike, mothers with sleeping babies and children with glazed eyes haunted with fear and excitement, clinging to their mums and dads.

I crept closer. From where I was standing, I could see the heaps of leaves the megapode bird had gathered to lay its eggs. 'I must be careful,' I warned myself, knowing that snakes crept into the nest. Some of these reptiles were as huge as my body.

Back in the village, in the Kibung, an argument broke out matching the velocity of the eruption itself. Some argued that this was a false alarm and the eruption was going to be manageable. Others felt that this was a big one and they should pack up and move immediately at first light. The arguments raged on deep into the night and early hours of the morning. In the distance, the rumbling kept up its tempo sending fear into many of the villagers' hearts.

I reached the foot of the oak trunk. Immediately I noticed that the nest was huge, bigger than many of the ones I had raided for eggs. Usually one bird lays up to 20 eggs if not disturbed, and I had a feeling this one would hold more eggs than I could carry. In my haste, I forgot to use the stick to poke around the nest. This was done to disturb the snakes and lizards that made the nest their homes. The warmth of the nest and heat rising from the volcano suited the reptiles and you would normally find a number of these slippery crawlers in the nest. I hated snakes and avoided them whenever I could.

I was very excited and I reached out with my bare hands to remove the outside layers of dirt and grass in the nest. I did that without problems. I dug further and further removing a number of layers of debris. Finally, my fingers touched something smooth and quickly I removed the last layers of grass.

The meeting came to a rowdy end with half the villagers voting to stay and the other half deciding to leave. Many argued that this was their home and they were afraid of moving to another location. They felt they would rather die here than leave their homes. But the local priest argued with the people and told them they can always come back. 'Friends, listen to me. If you live, you can always come back. If you die here, what's the point?' he asked solemnly.

'Father is right, friends,' said an old man as he stood up unsteadily. Willing hands tried to help him but he brushed these aside and stood tall. The people quietened down paying deep respect to the oldest man in the village. It was customary to respect the elders of the village without question. 'Father is right. I have had this bad feeling in my bones, lately. This one is a bad one. You should all pack up and leave first thing in the morning. Better to be alive than dead!'

'Wow!' I exclaimed as I saw the beautiful white eggs, stacked one on top of each other. They were huge—much larger than the ordinary fowl eggs I usually collected. I estimated there were over 100 eggs or more. I picked one up and boy it was heavy. This surprised me for megapode eggs were never that heavy.

Suddenly, I heard a dreadful sound behind me, then, 'Hissssesh! Hisses-ess-ss!' followed by a slithering noise. My blood turned cold and I shivered. I slowly turned around dreading what I would see. At first I could not see what had disturbed me and in my haste to turn around, I slipped and fell down.

'Oh, noooo!' I cried out, attempting to catch the egg. But it was out of my reach and I watched in horror as the egg sailed down. I knew it would smash. 'What a waste,' I thought angrily.

But just before the egg hit the root of the massive oak, something strange happened. Something caught the egg! I blinked my eyes, trying to catch a glimpse of the thing, refusing to believe what my mind was suggesting. At the same time, there was a dreadful cry of grief as if someone had lost a loved one. A feeling of dread engulfed me. Slowly, the hissing sound gained momentum, followed by a deafening noise. I hurriedly picked myself up and glanced up. My blood froze and I stood transfixed.

Coming towards me was the largest snake I had ever seen in my life. It was so huge: the eyes were the size of dinner plates and they were red hot. As I watched, mesmerised, the gigantic reptile slithered closer, its massive head only centimetres from my face. I stood immobile, paralysed by fear, unable to move or breathe. I was hypnotised as well by the snake's red hot eyes. I watched in horror as the reptile's long tongue flicked around my face, first one way and then the other, looking for any sign of fear.

I could feel the sweat running down, soaking me. I still did not move. I couldn't speak either. Once more the huge head with the hypnotic eyes circled around my face. For a minute we stood staring at each other, then it opened its huge mouth and again I gaped in horror at the huge tunnel. I could not see the end of the mouth, but one could drive a huge 10-tonne truck into that gaping passageway. I knew the reptile was going to swallow me.

Suddenly, something whistled past me with blinding speed and entered the gaping hole. A frantic battle began. I watched in amazement. Protruding from the creature's mouth was the giant oak tree. Its trunk was in the huge snake's mouth, but I watched in horror as the movement of the powerful snake caused the roots to come loose from the earth. They struggled on and on until I saw the old tree now with only its taper root for support.

The old tree trunk was communicating to me. It was telling me to run. But I knew I couldn't. I had to help him, my noble Oak tree. No longer was it just an ordinary tree. I knew that the spiritual Oak *was* my people's saviour and no matter what, I must help. In the frantic battle, one of the huge eggs had rolled down to my foot. Instinctively, I grabbed the egg and hurled it with all my strength at the reptile's eyes. The reptile saw it coming and tried to deflect my missile, but my aim was true. The huge egg shattered with a mighty bang on the snake's forehead, and the yellow slimy fluid poured into his eyes causing the snake to become blind. As I watched fascinated, smoke started pouring out of the reptile's eyes, and at the same time I felt a huge hand grab me and move me to safety.

Manam then erupted with a velocity that threatened to drown the island with hot lava, pyroclastic materials, gas and ashes.

'Asimba! Asimba! Stop screaming. It's me, Nazame, your mother. Come on wake up. We have to go. Manam has blown!' she cried shaking my shoulder.

I woke up with a start. I quickly crawled out of my bed sweating and quivering as if I had run a marathon. 'Mother— mother, what is the matter?' I cried out, hearing shouting and screaming from my neighbours. In the distance I could hear thunder rumbling but there was no rain. 'What's

happening, please someone tell me?' I yelled out as I went towards the voices of my family.

'Manam em i paia, Asimba. Mipela i mas go. Nao, hariap na bungiam ol klos bilong yu. Plis hariap!' ordered my father as he hurried off to supervise the packing.

'What?' I gasped. I stood still and examined myself. 'Was it only a dream or real?' I wondered. Then something itched in my left palm and I opened my hand. There was a miniature replica of an oak trunk in my hand, polished and shining. I knew. Without a word, I got up and packed my small possession. Once that was done, I went outside to help mother pack whatever we could carry. Dawn was breaking over the horizon and I could see that the wind would change directions soon. With that would come the smoke and ash.

'Are we ready?' asked father.

'Yes, we are all ready!' replied mother.

'Come, let us go!' and without turning his back, Asigo led our family out to the beach, where we would be evacuated to the mainland.

I did not move with the others immediately. The beach was only a few minutes away. My eyes roved to the mountain while unconsciously my fingers fidgeted the talisman hanging on my neck. A single tear dropped and touched the land; where my people had lived since time began. I heard the painful cries of my people mingled with fear and anger as they moved on. My heart was heavy.

'Thank you Oak tree. Thank you for saving the lives of my people!' I whispered softly. Then in a firm voice I whispered again, 'Mi bai kam bek!' and I vacated my family's home of 50 000 years—Manam Island.

Source: Picture drawn by Jake Kian in Grade 3B, 10 years old

The volcanic island of Manam

Manam is a beautiful island that lies off the coast of Madang town, facing north towards Bogia and East Sepik. It lies in the Bismarck Sea, which is part of the great Pacific Ocean. However, it is not an ordinary island. It is a volcanic island. This means the whole island sits on an active volcano. This lovely island has had its share of volcanic eruptions reaching back many thousand of years, perhaps 50 000 years. However, no one really knows how old Manam is.

A number of tribes have lived on the island since time began; for example, the Mangem to the north, the Asuramba to the east, and the Potsdam and Kuluguma to the south. The people are very friendly and there are hardly any law and order problems. Because the island is fertile, the people make gardens and feed off the land. They are also skilled fishermen who know the Bismarck Sea like the back of their hand. The people have been blessed and not many leave the island, unless for employment on the mainland.

Sadly, tragedy has struck this carefree island once again. On Sunday 24 October 2004, around 9 a.m., the volcano on Manam Island erupted, spurting molten lava and ashes and sending clouds of thick smoke 6000 metres high. This time the size of the eruption was bigger and the people of the island have been instructed to relocate to the mainland.

The northern part of Papua New Guinea, especially the islands and coastal regions like Manus, East and West New Britain, New Ireland, North Solomon's, Madang, Popondetta (mainland) and many other small islands, are products of extinct and active volcanoes.

The formation of volcanoes

An eruption
This is like a bottle of fizzy drink that has been shaken. If you shake the fizzy drink before opening it, there is a build up of gases with no way to escape, which ultimately leads to an explosion when you take the lid off.

Magma
The molten rock inside a volcano is called **magma**. The magma is under great pressure with no available exit, like the air in the fizzy drink bottle. If the amount of gas inside the volcano's magma is high, it has to get rid of the gas which leads to a massive explosion.

Manam Island
For a number of years, there had been a constant build up of gases inside the molten rock, and on Sunday 24 October 2004, it was time for it to blow up.

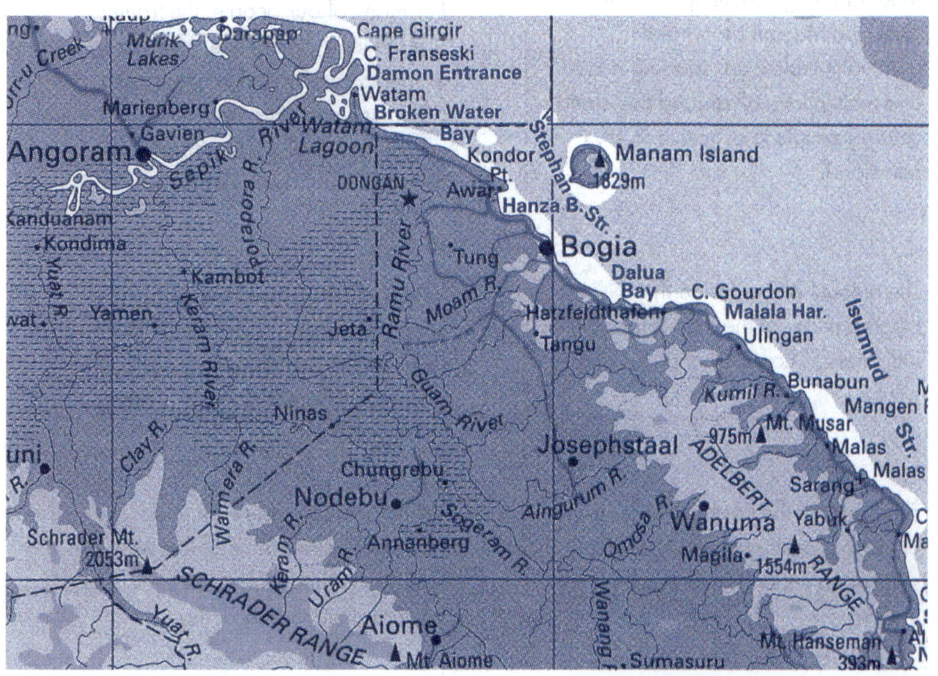

How do scientists work out how devastating a volcano will be?

Vulcanologists are people who study volcanoes.

The thickness of magma is also an important factor in telling us how active volcanoes are, and when one will erupt.

When the magma rises to what is called the lower pressures of the surface, the gases expand.

Magma and gas built up for three weeks on Manam Island and eventually it blew up, spurting gases and molten lava all around the island, causing people to evacuate their homeland.

The amount of gas inside the magma is one of the most important indicators to how violent an eruption will be.

The centre of the Earth is made up of magma, with numerous gases suspended under pressure in the magma.

Think of it like a balloon getting larger and larger when more air is pumped inside. Eventually, the expansion of air becomes too much and the balloon blows up.

Other volcanoes that have exploded in PNG are Mt Matupit and Tavurvur in Rabaul in 1993, Mt Ulamon in Hoskins in 1994 and Mt Lamington in Popondetta in 1951.

The deaths of people and destruction of properties have been devastating. For many of our people, the trauma is a life-long experience. Manam erupted in 1616 and has erupted 30 times since. This time 10 000 people got displaced and had to be relocated on the mainland.

When volcanoes erupt, they usually spurt a number of substances, like lava, pyroclastic materials, ash and gas, with different degrees of force.

When a volcano blew up, our ancestors believed the Spirits were angry with them and were punishing them for their wrong doings.

Lava is a liquefied rock. Imagine that you heated a rock (solid stone) and it turned into a liquid. This would be magma, and it would glow bright yellow, orange and red. It would be hotter than boiling water and it would give off tremendous heat—too much for anyone to withstand. If we were to go near the magma, we would get burnt by the terrific heat, and that is why a lot of people have to evacuate their lands.

The **magma chamber** is where the molten rock builds up under the earth. When the gases expand with pressure, the molten rock, gas and smoke travel up the main vent and out through the crater.

Today with modern technology, vulcanologists can tell us when a volcano is likely to erupt. With such warning, our people can move away from the danger area.

The smoke and gas are blown by the wind for miles around the island or land and these can be dangerous too. The molten lava flows down the side of the mountain, damaging land, homes and streams. That is what happened to Manam Island.

But even with this modern technology, we are never sure when Mama Graun decides to send a calling card.

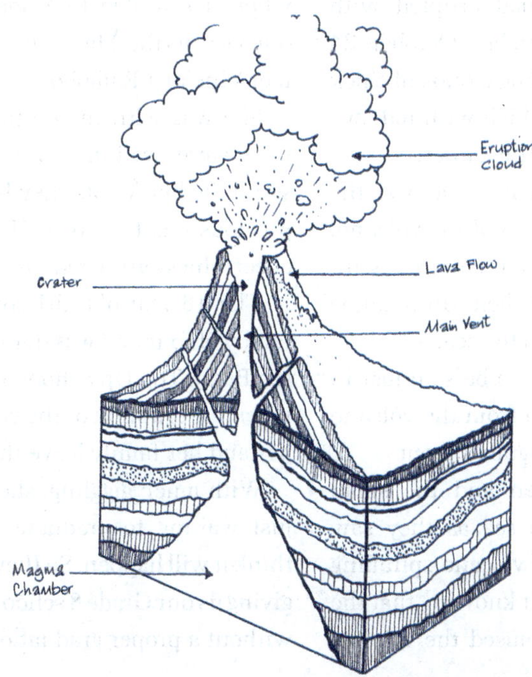

Human face of Manam Island

Wanita Wakus

AS THE MEN, women and children walked to the *MV Motuan Chief* an elderly man came down, stood at the wharf and looked back towards the island and began crying.

It was the wailing of a man whose heart had been torn out by the fact he would be leaving the place of his ancestors, the graves of his loved ones and the place where he had for all his life called home. He would have to settle on a land that would be on a temporary basis or for the rest of his life until he closes his eye to say goodbye to the world.

The volcano on Manum Island in Madang Province had erupted with a huge bang on Sunday, October 24 – around 9am, sending clouds of thick smoke 6000 metres high with red lava spewing down from the crater.

A mother was at home and at the sound of the explosion of the volcano, she prepared her four children with her small baby, put them on a canoe and sent them out to the sea.

She wanted them to be safe just in case the red hot lava from the volcano flowed down and engulfed them.

The four children and the small baby drifted out to sea as they saw the smoke from the volcano spiralling high into the sky, not knowing that the eruption had also caused the tides to swell and the sea began to get rough.

Trying to paddle and keep within the vicinity of the island, the wind and the swelling waves swept their small canoe out further away from the island.

Fortunately, the wind had swept them towards the mainland and some villagers on the mainland in Bogia who had also heard the huge eruption from the volcano saw them. So they went out and rescued the young.

It has been a month and two weeks now and still the volcano is giving out smoke and small amounts of lava are still flowing out of the volcano.

My trip was made possible by the UNICEF child protection and nutrition and health officers with whom I travelled to Madang. During our visit to the Mangem care centre, I met Vinciana Raibobo.

She was with three other girls and they were walking to the beach to scrub the black pots they had used the previous night to cook. Her smile and cheerfulness attracted my attention.

The 16-year-old girl comes from a family of four and was doing Grade 8 at the Biang Top Up School on the island when the eruption of the volcano made her and her family leave the island.

With much giggling, she said: "I am just waiting to graduate but I don't think it will happen. So they will just be giving us our Grade 8 school certificates without a proper graduation."

"We were lucky to have our exams before they declared a stage-three alert and we had to be evacuated."

Without any expression on her face she looked out into the ocean and said: "I am sad that we have left the island but I don't know if we'll ever return to the island."

For the young children, it is an adventure and a new experience they are encountering. But for the older people, the island holds a lot of things for them.

It holds the memories of their youth, adventures and the memories of their loved ones who they have laid to rest. Not only that, but it also holds their identity, their origin of existence.

Whether the people will return back to there is something that only Heaven knows.

The picture below shows the Manam volcano blowing its top.

The people from Kuluguma getting off the *MV Motuan Chief* to be resettled at one of the three care centres.

The resettled people at the care centre try to start a new life with the building of a home.

Despite the heartaches of the elders, the children have fun on the beach of their new home.

Children stand to see the mudslide caused by the volcano flowing out into the sea.

Things to do after reading

Complete the following activities after you have read the passage. They will help you understand more about the formation and eruption of volcanoes in Papua New Guinea, especially the island volcanoes like Manam.

Activity 1

Think about the people of Manam. How do you think they felt when they were told to evacuate their island home? For some this was the only home they had known all their lives. To leave their homes without knowing whether they would ever return would have been heartbreaking, wouldn't it?

1. Write a short story about how you and your family escaped the molten lava, ash or gases. Express how sad you feel.
2. Write a poem or a diary entry to explore your feelings about the day the actual eruption began or the day your family had to escape.
3. Write a letter to the people of Manam expressing how you as an outsider feel about the loss of their homes and land.

Activity 2

Imaginative extension

Imagine you are Asimba and you have come back to the island after some years living elsewhere. What are you going to do? Write the role of the Old Oak Tree, The Giant Reptile, Manam the volcano or Asimba.

Exposition

6

Dream a pot of green gold

I was glad that the National Grade 6 Examination was over. I had made plans to visit my cousins in Talaseia, but my class teacher had asked us to stay back. Usually, I would have stayed away from school but my uncle Eka had threatened not to pay for the trip if I didn't finish school. So reluctantly, I attended the final weeks of school.

Mr Sei was my class teacher and he was a nice man. In fact, he was the best teacher I had ever had and so this Friday 16 September, 2004 while my mind was already in Talaseia, West New Britain Province, my body sat in class. And as you can understand, only fragments of the teacher's talk filtered through my drowsy brain.

'You don't have to spend your holidays—But plant—Orchid—Vanilla—uh? It's now becoming the export commodity, worth more than gold.'

What was Mr Sei up to? Doesn't he know that we are finished from this school? Our school days are over—finished—understood, uh? A part of me was awake listening to the gentle voice of my favourite teacher, but the other half of my being was across the vast Pacific Ocean, travelling far and wide, into coastal villages with cool ocean breezes, swaying palms trees and white coral sandy beaches.

'Kipi, are—?' Uh, who was that? Why bother me, eh?

'Kipi, are you listening?' Yeah, that sounds like my teacher.

'Look at that smile, sir. He is in dreamland,' a student must have been pointing his finger at me. I could hear chairs scrape on the wooden floor as students stood up to see me.

'Yep, that's for sure. He's far gone into another world. Ahiee, Kipi the dreamer,' teased Pearl my cousin.

I heard laughter and giggles from the girls.

'Teacher, em silip pinis!' sounded Nopa Raki. His voice is so near—but I'm not here. I am miles and miles away, riding the Highlands Highway.

The huge Toyota coaster bus is travelling down the famous Okuk highway at break-neck speed. I watch amazed at the countryside, the famous Wahgi Valley speeding past my window. I catch only slight glimpses of coffee plantations, tea factories, villages, landscapes and people waving at us. My adventure has begun.

Our first stop is a town call Chimbu and I look out the window with wonder. I see over a million people on the streets. Everywhere I look there are people of all races: white, brown, black and even yellow-skinned people. Some young, some old, men, women, children and young people alike. The street is packed with people and then I encounter the peddlers—the street vendors. Oh, my goodness they storm the bus. One of them, a youth my own age, pops up to me with a couple of cheese pop packets and waves them in my face yelling, 'Fifty toea! Fifty toea each!' Very soon, the whole bus is crowded with street vendors peddling all kinds of wares: soft drinks, food and cigarettes, some even come with second-hand clothes.

'Em K2 tasol, yia. Buyim pren?' the second-hand clothes peddler offers one of the passengers in the front row. Even though the man is not interested, the peddler tries his best to convince the passenger. He has good persuasive skills and the man eventually buys the shirts and immediately another seller turns up with a different shirt.

'Simuk for 30 toea tasol,' calls one of the smoke sellers. I look at these street sellers with interest and wonder. But hey, I think we have been doped.

If we had been watching carefully, we might have picked up the plot but alas it's too late. I am taught my first lesson.

'Hey, Kipi. Watch our bag,' calls Uncle Eka as he stands up. He must have anticipated something.

I am too busy looking at these street peddlers. They are really amazing, uh? 'Man, at least they are trying to make a living but how long can they last? And is this the best choice they could make?' I ask myself. 'How much would they make a day, anyway?'

Suddenly, one of the passengers in the 25-seater coaster bus yells, 'Em stilim bek biling mi. He has stolen my bag,' and tries to chase the youth. But too late, the crook disappears among the crowd. Perhaps not all of the youths were striving for a living by peddling. Some of them were there for dubious reasons. Though angered by this event I feel sad for the youths. This is my generation, and we have taken a wrong footing—we've made poor choices. The role the poor youth (thief) has chosen is not a good one. Yeah, the youth had the choice: right or wrong, good or evil, honest or dishonest, but I realise the young man has made a poor choice of occupation, one that will eventually lead him to prison. Sure, it's easy money but stolen things never last. And the lad has broken the law. Not worth the risk, I figure. Taking the incident as a warning, the driver starts the bus and we fly away.

In the class, the conversation about me was still continuing. Not often do we perform actions while in dreamland but I must be putting a good show.

'His mind is already in Rabaul,' said Koni Wek, and again there was laughter.

'Not Rabaul, silly,' corrected Agnes Maip. 'It's Talaseia in West New Britain!' More laughter was heard and plenty of giggles. Footsteps were coming my way but my body wouldn't respond. I am already in Goroka.

This is the next bus stop we have reached. We travel past the winding and twisting Chimbu and Sinasina gorge. I have noticed a lot of people living along the highway. Wow, the food gardens on the side of the cliffs, hills and mountains are amazing. The people know how to use the land, except that I hardly see any trees growing along the highway, nor the hills. Uncle Eka must have read my mind for he says, 'The people have cut down all the trees and bushes for gardening, Kipi. The population of Chimbu is rapidly increasing. There is not enough land. That's why you see barren land on the sides of mountains, where once there was a huge forest.'

'Uncle, why can't they plant trees, like we do at home? This will allow the forests to grow again, won't it?' I ask, puzzled. Back home we have a tree-planting project running with the forestry department. I have personally planted 20 trees.

'Yes, they could but the people either don't know or don't want to. I don't know, Kipi. But we're already here in Goroka.'

Yeah, we have, for I could see the huge sign reading 'Welcome to Goroka town.' Immediately, I notice that here the place is much more peaceful. No one rushes the bus with wares. It's not like Chimbu. The people calmly stand and watch us. The crewmember of the bus calls out for passengers travelling to Lae to come on board. This is a pick-up zone. Oh, the next stop will be in Lae.

'Uncle, have we passed the Kassam Pass yet?' I ask yawning. We must have travelled for six hours or so and I am tired.

'No, not yet. We passed the Daulo Pass some kilometres back but Kassam Pass is on the boarder of Lae and Goroka. Come, you sleep. I'll wake you at Kassam—' but I am long gone into my new world.

'All right, pupils. Perhaps this will wake him up?' and the teacher placed something on the table. It is two large brown rectangle boxes.

'Oh, great teacher. We love you teacher. You're the greatest!' the students yelled and clapped their hands in anticipation. I heard chairs scrape as students hurriedly stand up or move. But, where? I heard no bell! I didn't know what it is that the teacher has unwrapped. But I was not interested.

'Hmm-mmm-mma! That's delicious. What flavour, Sir?' The children seem to know what's in the boxes.

I have never been to Talaseia or for that matter to Lae or any other city in Papua New Guinea. Part of my planned trip is on a boat called *MV Rita* and I will travel across the Pacific Ocean to Kimbe.

Hey wait. Did I smell something? Yes, I did and my nostrils start to flare. Hey, that couldn't be. It smells like—uh? Oh, never mind, look at that lovely beach and oh boy, what a beautiful ocean.

'Kipi? Mr Kipi!'

Was the teacher calling my name? Uh, why would he?—Uh, I'm no longer in school.

Ohooo, this feels good—uh. I smile for this is the kind of life I want to live. I am running along a beautiful white sandy beach that seems to go on for miles and miles. I laugh with glee, enjoying the rusty feel of the sand. I touch the gently rolling crystal clear waters, reaching out like a giant hand to greet me, allowing the wet silky feeling to wash over me.

Oh, that's a delicious smell—I couldn't be smelling my—uh? My nostrils started twisting on their own free will again. I heard laughter too.

'Man bilong smelim ol something i kiraip pinis. Lukim em!' said Freeman grinning.

There were giggles all around. The teacher cleared his throat. 'Kipi, are you awake, now? If you are, come and get some ice-cream, please?'

Ice-cream? Yeah, that was what I had got a whiff of? Oh, my favourite. My eyes popped open and all the children laughed. I hung my heard shyly. I released a deep sigh pondering, 'Oh, was it only a dream?'

'Kipi, you can be the first as you are going away. This is part of the lesson I was giving you all this week. It's also my present to you children for being such wonderful pupils. I've had a great year. Thanks for your support and cooperation—' Mr Sei said almost in tears.

The children all clapped and some shed tears. The girls weeped openly and waited for me. I gently pulled my chair back and walked to the front of the class feeling guilty. I had not understood a word Mr Sei had been saying all week. As I was walking up, Mr Sei must have sensed my turmoil and boy, did he help out? To this day, I owe my gratitude and future to my favourite teacher, Mr Sei.

'Pupils, the ice-cream you are going to eat is made using an ingredient from the vanilla plant we have been discussing. As you come and get your ice cream, take a look at these beans. They are vanilla beans, ready for selling and as you can smell the aroma, it is the same as the ice-cream we will have.' Mr Sei told the students.

I finally made my way up to the front and turned to face the pupils. I cleared my throat and the teacher again sensed my mood. 'I think Mr Kipi wants to say something. Let's give him our attention, please?' We shook hands and hugged each other, and I tried not to cry.

'Thank you Mr Sei,' I nodded in his direction. 'Friends, first of all I want to apologise for sleeping in class—' there was laughter from the children but they quietened down immediately. 'Mr Sei, can you hand me those vanilla beans, please?' I held up the bunch of beans.

'Students, look at these? Do you realise that this bunch of brown beans is worth K700–900 per kilo? And it comes from this plant called vanilla?' I hold up the vanilla cutting the teacher had been using. 'Well friends, I am going to plant this crop in Talaseia. My uncle has a block of land and he has especially asked me to come and help him plant and look after the plot. That is why I am going on such a long journey. You see, vanilla can grow here in the Highlands but it will take a long time to flower—'

I educated the students about the crop as an export commodity; a way of making a living or business opportunity for an individual and a chance to help PNG bring in foreign currency. All the talk the teacher had been dishing to us over the week I presented in another way and the children sat still, listening in wonder. 'So friends, we must work for ourselves so that we can put food on the table. Who knows, in a number of years time, you and I can become millionaires, eh? It is a matter of making the right choice in our lives. If we make the wrong choice, we will regret it to the day we die. So children, when we leave school, we must make the right choice on what we need to do with our lives.'

There was no laughter. The topic had sobered the children up and given them food for thought. Mr Sei stared at me in wonder. He came forward and shook my hand. 'Mr Kipi, now I know why you dream all day. Go and make your dreams a reality, my son. I give you all my blessing and I know God will make your dreams come true!'

I thanked him and within a week, Eka and I took a bus to Lae, boarded *MV Rita* and landed in Kimbe two days later. From then on I never looked back. I made an informed choice for my future and built my dreams by hard work. I made my own future through difficult times and became a millionaire. Vanilla was my pot of gold, a story of a Papua New Guinean who made it through personal sacrifice and hard work. For me, the sky was the limit. I had made the right choice with God and was blessed abundantly!

Mama Graun: the natural giver of life

Do you realise that Mama Graun takes care of her own? Humans cut the trees down for logging and unnecessarily burn up the grass and savannah grasslands. When mining for natural treasures, we damage the land, sometimes so extensively that animals or plant life can no longer survive on such barren land. This is sad, and it is a fact that if PNG continues to flout our natural resources such as timber, gold, copper, oil, fish and the other treasures of this beautiful island country, in the next century we will face a drastic shortage.

It is our responsibility today to rationalise our natural resources, especially those resources that are sustainable or renewable. A small tree-planting project, which kicked off in the Wahgi Valley in Mt Hagen, promises to provide income for young school leavers for many years and at the same time it will provide timber for power pavilions and building constructions. People living along the Wahgi Valley have benefited from this project. The villagers have been issued seedlings from the Exculpates (Gum) tree and have planted their own. Soon, many people will have trees to sell or will be able to build their

houses with the wood from these trees. Exculpates trees grow fast. In many parts of the country, soil and climatic conditions are conducive for these trees to grow.

Tree planting is a renewable resource. When you cut down a tree, you must plant a young tree beside the one you have cut. This way the young tree replaces the one you have chopped down. Today, logging is damaging vast areas of forest in PNG, leaving many areas wasteland. Take for example the Tomba area, which borders Western Highlands and the Enga province. This is one such wasteland (which is caused by the destruction of forest through logging), slowly deteriorating into savannah grassland. And of course, with the destruction of the forests, the animals and the beautiful flora go too. These forests, animals and plants were once a trademark of this scenic island paradise.

From the many gifts that Mama Graun offers, there is one crawling plant that is rapidly becoming a household name in many parts of Papua New Guinea. This can be an export commodity for our people. But like all the natural gifts offered by Mama Graun, they need proper management and care. This crawling plant will replace the Red or Yellow Gold we burrow from the depth of the earth, which is unfortunately non-renewable. But for now, let us study this beautiful golden green plant.

Vanilla: the Green Gold

Vanilla is one of Papua New Guinea's marketable commodities

The vanilla plant belongs to the family of orchids.

The Vanilla orchid (family—*Orchidaceae*) is also known as *Vanilla planifolia* or *Vanilla fragrans*, which are common species found in Mexico.

There are two varieties in PNG too: *Vanilla planifolia* and *Vanilla tahitensis*. These are found in many lowlands and coastal regions of PNG.

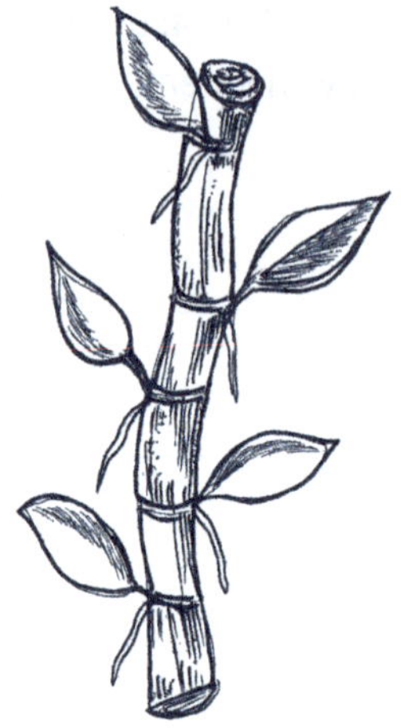

Vanilla is also called 'Green Gold' because for Grade 'A' vanilla beans, the price was around K700–900 per kilo in 2003.

Many Papua New Guineans are now planting and cultivating vanilla, but because they are not curing the beans properly the prices have dropped. Now the price is K50–150 per kilo beans.

It is still an important cash crop for the smaller-holder farming sector.

Vanilla grows from the cuttings of the vanilla orchid (crawling) plant.

This picture shows how a vanilla cutting can be planted. The cutting is planted near a growing tree. The short end with the bud is planted in the soil and the long stalk is tied to the tree.

The best tree to tie the vanilla to is a *Gliricidia* tree. For best results, some people plant the trees in advance and when the trees start to grow, the vanilla plant is planted beside them.

It takes about 24 months for well-managed vanilla plants to grow and flower. It is very important to clean and take care of the vanilla plant as it is a crawling plant, and if one is not careful, the shoots may grow in different directions or too high, causing problems for manual pollination of the flowers. This takes a lot of work.

Pruning and looping the vanilla plant

In the next series of work in grade 7, you will read about pollinating flowers, harvesting, curing and grading the vanilla beans before they are sold for money. The value of the beans depends on the curing process. You get better returns if this is done well. If not, you get what you deserve.

A short history of vanilla

pre-Columbian times	the Mayans and Aztecs used vanilla to flavour chocolate drinks.
1600s	famous Spanish navigator Herman Cortes was the first to discover and bring the vanilla plant to Europe.
19th century	the plant was not cultivated domestically until the 19th century by a slave named Edmond Albius. Albius lived on the French island of Réunion, near Madagascar in Africa. He was the first person to manually pollinate the vanilla flower.
Present	Madagascar is the leading vanilla producing country in the world.

Things to do after reading

Activity 1

Vanilla or Tree-planting Project

The school could do a vanilla project if you are from the lowlands or coastal regions where vanilla suits your soil and climatic conditions. If you are from the Highlands, I suggest an exculpates (gum) tree-planting project. For proper management purposes, the project should be small, say 50 vanilla plants. The more you plant, the harder it is to manage. Even 50 vanilla plants may be too large. But the option is there for the school to start a self-help project that in the long run will yield some good returns for the school.

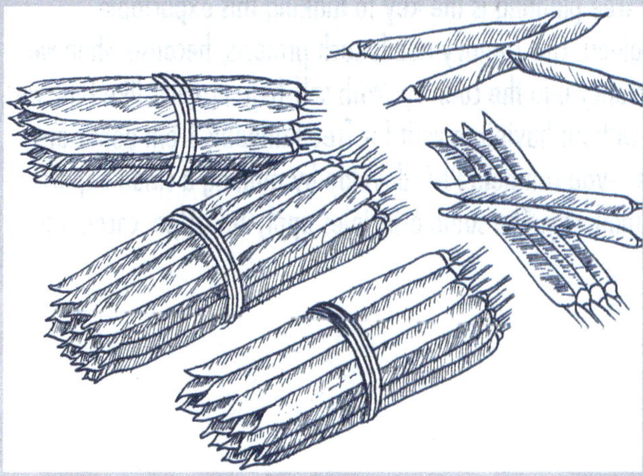

Activity 2

Individual student projects are also possible. One can plant 20 vanilla plants in one central location. You can cultivate these plants each week/month to make sure that there is enough mulch around the plants to keep the soil moisture up. Things you could use to mulch the plants include coconut husks, banana fruit, pawpaw, water-melon and pumpkin skins as well as vegetable waste. You can also use fertiliser. Seek help from your local Department of Agriculture & Livestock Division (DAL) officer.
You need to constantly weed.

Then as the vanilla plant starts to crawl up the support tree, you need to loop the vines to reachable heights, so as not to let them grow wildly. You need the vanilla vines within arms reach, so that you can hand pollinate the flowers when they bloom.

Activity 3

Find more information about vanilla. Then, with the help of your teacher, go to the villages to educate the people about vanilla. You can use posters, information leaflets, pamphlets and tapes. Such an activity may need a lot of planning and help from your local DAL officer.

Activity 4

Write a story about your vanilla or tree-planting project for the local newspaper. Newspapers are interested in promoting self-help projects initiated by individuals and organisations such as schools.

Educating our people about vanilla or tree planting is the key to making this exportable commodity a success in Papua New Guinea. Our country needs such projects, because when we export, we are bringing in foreign currency into the country. With self-help projects like this, we can help our country develop further without having to wait for free handouts from politicians and the government. Think about this—you can help PNG develop by making a small export-driven contribution, even if it is in a small way. The same principles apply to coffee, cocoa, oil palm, rubber and copra.

7 Poetry

Mama Graun (Creation and Death)

By Mulzi Nalaye

Mama Graun, Mama Graun,
Oh, mother of the rainbow colours,
Beautiful black, yellow, white, and brown,
Mama, the colour of the rainbows,
You know no colour difference.
Mama Graun, you brought me forth,
You fed me,
You clothed me,
I knew no one but you.
You moulded me and
You gave me life.
Mama Graun, you for me,
I for you,
Without you, I no live.
I depend on you,
You depend on me,
Without me, you no more,
We are two of a kind.
I embrace your beautiful bosom,
Like a baby suckling her mother's breast.
You feed me, clothe and shelter me,

Mama Graun,
You for me
And I for you,
We are, but one.
Mama Graun,
I await your final call
To thy elegant bosom,
To take refuge one last time.
And wait for the mighty one
who moulded me out of you,
To mail the calling card,
To go places afar.
Till then, Mama Graun,
You keep the faith and
Hold unto your bosom,
Thy creation in trust,
for all Eternity.

A Ballad of Papua

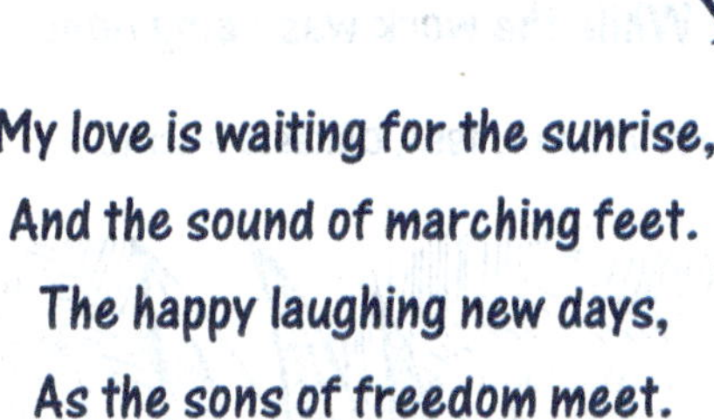

Josephine Abaijah

My love is waiting for the sunrise,
And the sound of marching feet.
The happy laughing new days,
As the sons of freedom meet.
Chorus
Paradise bird you're fly-ing;
Yellow cap and band of gold.
Paradise bird you're cry-ing;
Summer wings on lilac fold.
Redder bird you're dy-ing;
Redder than the blushing sky,
Carried in a lover's sigh,
As dreaming times go drifting by,
With mem-or-ies of Pa-pu-ah.
My love is waiting for Pa-pu-ah,
For the thunder of the drums,
To roll from sea to mountain,
When the victory has been won.
My love is waiting for toiling,
And the planting of the seed.
The axe and kai-ah ringing,

As we fill our nation's need.
My love is waiting for the praying,
The joy and sweat and tears.
As growing up together,
We sing away the years.
My love is waiting for the dreaming,
And the setting of the sun.
For the hearts that beat together,
While the work was being done.

from *A thousand coloured dreams*, 1991, Dellasta Pacific

Respect the Jungle: A jungle fable

Day 1

Three friends one day set out into the jungle
To gather wild mushrooms.
Upon arrival they began to set up camp.

The first man's task was to collect
Firewood for the fire.
He collected enough for one day.
The second man's job was to fetch water
He fetched enough for two days.
The third person's job was to
Build a shelter.
He looked up into the sky
And saw that the weather was fine.
Grinning he took a nap.

Dreaming away he forget his task
Awakened rudely by a fly,
Sailing up his tunnel of air,
Threatening to enter his windbag.
Yelling, with fright, he stood,

Only to find a young kunai shoot
Had entered his feet.

'Aiyee husssh, Aiyee hush!' he cried,
And hopped to an old tree trunk.
But as soon as he sat, he sat bolt up right,
Shaking his lakaup to free the mighty red ant
Who gritted its teeth into tender flesh,
Not letting go until the man stood
As naked as the day he was born.

'Aiyee hush,' he cried.
'Why me, to be beaten and eaten?'
Painfully he recalled his task and
Hastily built a crude shelter.

In the evening, the friends all met
And gathering around the new shelter
Cooked their evening meals.
They ate, drank and slept.

Day 2

The next day, the three friends all
Went out gathering mushrooms.
They travelled east, west and north
And as the evening was drawing
Nearer, they headed south,
For home—of course loaded.

That night, they burnt all the firewood,
Drank most of the water
And feasted on mushrooms.
In the evening they moved outside,
The night was fine
And it promised
A wonderful day for travelling home.

Day 3

Early next morning, the friends' cooked,
Ate and drank the last of the water.
'Hey, don't drink all the water!' said the first man.
'Why?' asked the second man, 'we are going home!'
The third man looked up in the sky,
It promised another fine day.
'Yeah, we're going home! Drink up
And pour the rest away.
There is plenty on the way home!'

Excited about going home,
They threw the remaining food away,
Pulled the house apart,
Destroyed the fire by peeing and
Putting excreta into the fireplace.
'Hey, don't do that!' the first man objected.
But laughing excitedly, he too followed his friends
And laughing with mirth, they set off for home.
The friends travelled fast
But strangely, they went nowhere.
The sun shone very brightly,
The three men felt thirsty.
'Hey any water?' asked the first man.
'Nooo!' the two other men replied together.
They licked dry lips and struggled on.
Their bags full with mushrooms.

About midday, the sky turned inwards,
In the distance it rumbled,
And the wind began howling.
The friends looked at each other,
Shaking their heads.
'Can we make it, home?
No, we can't. The storm's coming and—'
They headed back.

As they did, heaven opened it doors
And a baptism of rain smothered
The friends in the blink of an eye.
Old jungle folk saying,
Beware of the Yuukati (lightening)
But who listens when the jungle calls.

The third man carrying his bag,
Runs under a Taro tree for shelter,
Unheeding shouts of warning.
Next minute, a huge flash
Of lightening strikes the tree.
Only the bag remains,
The third man, no more,
Only a burned up corpse.

Two friends mourn but can't cry,
Howling wind blows their sorrows away.
From everywhere water rushes in all
Directions, causing mud banks,
And trees fall down inches from their feet.

Lightning flashes angrily, again and again,
Causing each man to grab a helping hand,
They head for the makeshift shelter.

They seem lost, bloodshot eyes,
Skin torn by falling branches,
And knees scraped and bleeding,
They find their home.

Miraculously, some of the shelter
Is still intact and dry.
When they enter, it dawns on them.
They look at each other.
Neither hesitating, their hands scrape the fireplace
Sodden with fresh shit.
They clean it up and light a fire.

Angrily the storm howls
Through the night, day and night,
Weeping through the gorges and valleys
Carrying a message of death.
The crude fire glows, for a minute
It looks like the flame would catch on.
But like a flaming candle,
The light snaps out,
For there was no firewood.

It begins to get cold,
At the same time the sky darkened,
And the forests close in
The two pay no heed.

For warmth, the two men
Embrace like lovers,
And thus they were found
Many, many years later.
The forest had laid claim to its trespassers.

Manam Island

Manam, for 50 000 years,
You have been my refuge,
My anchor, my roots, my lover.
Manam, 50 000 years
I have held on to your bosoms
Like a blood-sucking leach,
I have lived, reproduced and
Raised my multitudes of generations.
Manam, my beloved Island,
My hearts weeps in agony.
Chorus
Manam, Why? I cry,
Manam, Why? I weep.
Why? I ponder, Why? I ask,
Are you severing the
50 000-year-old umbilical cord?
Manam, my beautiful island home,
Island of swaying palm trees,
Beautiful coral reefs
As clear as crystal,
Beaches un-deflowered,
Gently flowing rivers and streams,
Forests still intact like a virgin

Manam, my first love, why?
Repeat chorus
Manam, your anger knows no limits,
But our love shall endure for all eternity,
Manam, my love, my home.
My heart quivers and shivers,
As I travel to distant lands,
A naked shell of a being only,
For my heart I leave behind.
Repeat chorus
Manam, my lover for 50 000 years,
You tried your best to divorce me,
But Manam, my love,
I will be back in the twinkle of an eye.
For this is not goodbye
But bon voyage,
We shall meet again.

Word list

active volcano
adventure
beautiful
breeze
chuckle
clash
crater
deafening
describe
destination
destroy
destructive
devastating
different
disbelieve
displace
erupt
evacuate
expansion
experience
extinct volcano
formation
form
gas
gigantic
gossip
haste
indicate
inhabit
innocent
journey
lava
magma
massive
mesmerise
modern technology
molten rock
murdering
numerous
peaceful
pressure
puzzle
quiet
reach
reply
reptile
route
silently
slithering
speechless
splash
spurting
study
suddenly
surface
surprise
suspend
temperament
thought
thunder
tickling
tributary
ultimately
understand
velocity
viscosity
volcanic island
volcano
vulcanologist